Drupal 5 Themes

Create a new theme for your Drupal website with
a clean layout and powerful CSS styling

D1319382

Ric Shreves

PUBLISHING

BIRMINGHAM - MUMBAI

Drupal 5 Themes

Create a new theme for your Drupal website with a clean layout and powerful CSS styling

First published: December 2007

Production Reference: 1171207

Published by Packt Publishing Ltd.
32 Lincoln Road
Olton
Birmingham, B27 6PA, UK.

ISBN 978-1-847191-82-3

www.packtpub.com

Cover Image by Vinayak Chittar (vinayak.chittar@gmail.com)

Credits

Author

Ric Shreves

Reviewer

Dave Myburgh

Senior Acquisition Editor

Douglas Paterson

Development Editor

Rashmi Phadnis

Technical Editor

Ajay S.

Editorial Manager

Dipali Chittar

Project Manager

Patricia Weir

Indexer

Hemangini Bari

Proofreaders

Harminder Singh

Chris Smith

Production Coordinator

Aparna Bhagat

Shantanu Zagade

Cover Designer

Aparna Bhagat

About the Author

Ric Shreves is a partner in water & stone (www.waterandstone.com), a web development company that specializes in open-source content management systems. He works primarily as a consultant and business systems analyst and is currently on extended assignment with Peace Dividend Trust. He lives in Bali with his wife Nalisa, one dog, two cats, three turtles, and a mind-boggling number of fish.

First and foremost, I thank my loving wife Nalisa for her support and patience. It would also be remiss of me to fail to acknowledge my friend (and editor at ComputerWorld) Stefan Hammond, who provides more than a modicum of support and encouragement — together with much-needed reality checks.

About the Reviewer

Dave Myburgh started out in computers when entire operating systems ran on a single floppy disk and 640kb of RAM was a lot! He studied to become a molecular biologist, but never lost his passion for computers. Later, he ran a successful computer company for a couple of years in South Africa, before moving to Canada with his wife. He went back to science on his arrival in Canada, and since discovering Drupal almost two years ago, he has once again started his own company, MybesInformatik. He loves working with Drupal, and is quite handy at theming, as well as hacking modules to make them do what he wants (sometimes, patches even get submitted back to the community). Now, he divides his time — unevenly — between family and Drupal.

I would like to thank Dries and the Drupal community for making Drupal what it is today. Without you guys and gals, I'd probably still be "doing static" — I can't wait for Drupal 6! I'd also like to thank my wife for putting up with my frequent late nights in front of the computer. I tell her it's work, but in reality, it's a lot of fun — just don't tell her I told you that.

Table of Contents

Preface   1

Chapter 1: The Elements of a Drupal Theme   5
What is a Theme?   5
What is a Templating Engine?   6
The Range and Flexibility of Drupal Themes   7
What You See on the Screen   8
The Big Picture: How Drupal Displays a Page   10
The Importance of Themes in Drupal   12
  Key Concepts   12
    Build with Blocks   14
    Intercept and Override   16
The Contents of the Drupal Distro   17
The Theme Files   21
  The Files of a PHPTemplate Theme   22
  The Files of a Pure PHP Theme   23
Summary   24

Chapter 2: Theme Set Up and Configuration   25
Finding Additional Themes   25
Installing an Additional Theme   28
Configuring a Theme   32
  Theme-Specific Configuration Options   33
  Global Configuration Settings   37
Managing Modules and Blocks   38
  The Module Manager   38
  The Blocks Manager   40
  Adding PHP to Blocks   45
Theming in Action: Dressing Up Garland   47
  Set the Color Scheme   48

Change Display Settings   49
Upload Logo   50
Global Configuration   50
Enable Modules   52
Manage Blocks   53
Add Some Dummy Content and Links   54
Set Access Levels   54
Create a Custom Block   55
Set Block Visibility   56
Uninstalling Themes   **60**
Summary   **60**

Chapter 3: Working with Theme Engines   **61**
What is PHPTemplate?   **61**
How does it Work?   **62**
Getting Started with PHPTemplate   **65**
A Look at the Theme Engine Files   66
A Look at the Key PHPTemplate File Contained in the Theme   **71**
Two Contrasting Examples   77
A Basic PHPTemplate Theme—Gagarin   78
A More Complex PHPTemplate Theme—Garland   78
Alternative Theme Engines   **80**
PHPTAL   80
Smarty   81
PHP XTemplate   81
Installing Additional Theme engines   **82**
Summary   **82**

Chapter 4: Style Sheets and Themeable Functions   **83**
A Guide to Drupal Style Sheets   **83**
Identifying Themeable Functions   **86**
A Guide to Themeable Functions   **87**
Aggregator Module Functions   87
Block Module Functions   88
Book Module Functions   88
Color Module Functions   88
Comment Module Functions   88
Drupal Module Functions   90
Filter Module Functions   90
Form Functions   90
Forum Module Functions   92

Locale Functions   92
Menu Functions   93
Node Module Functions   93
Pagination Functions   94
Poll Module Functions   94
Profile Module Functions   95
Search Module Functions   95
System Module Functions   96
Taxonomy Module Functions   96
Theme Functions   97
Upload Module Functions   99
User Module Functions   99
Watchdog Module Functions   100
Summary   **100**

Chapter 5: Intercepts and Overrides   **101**
Overriding the Default CSS   **101**
CSS Overrides in Action   103
Overriding Functions   **105**
Where to Place Overrides   106
How to Name Your Overrides   107
Overrides in Action: How Garland Works   108
Intercepting PHPTemplate Files   109
Overriding Themeable Functions in Garland   110
Various Approaches to Overrides   111
Intercepting and Substituting Files   111
Placing Overrides in the Theme's template.php File   112
Modifying the PHPTemplate Engine Files   113
Placing Overrides in Dedicated Files   113
Intercepting Template Files   **116**
Summary   **117**

Chapter 6: Modifying an Existing Theme   **119**
Setting Up the Workspace   **119**
Planning the Modifications   **120**
Cloning a Theme   **122**
First Look at Zen/Tao   **123**
CSS in Zen/Tao   123
Themeable Functions in Zen/Tao   126
Turning Zen into Tao   **127**
Configuring the Theme   127
Set Global and Theme Configuration Options   128
Enable Modules   128
Set User Access   129

Create Dummy Content	129
Set Up Menus	129
Add New Regions	131
Enable and Configure Blocks	133
Position Blocks	134
Adapting the CSS	135
Setting the Page Dimensions	136
Formatting the New Regions	136
Fonts and Colors	137
Formatting the Sidebars and Footer	140
Formatting the Menus	141
Formatting the Search Box	142
Formatting the Comments Form and Output	143
Adapting the Themeable Functions	144
Modifying template.php	144
Creating a New Template File	145
Before and After	147
Summary	**148**
Chapter 7: Building a New Theme	**149**
Planning the Build	**149**
Build a New PHPTemplate Theme	**152**
Building a page.tpl.php File	153
Insert DocType and Head	156
Insert Body Tags	157
Lay Out the Page Divisions	158
Place the Functional Elements	158
The Final page.tpl.php File	165
The style.css File	169
A Look at Our New Theme	178
Extending Your PHPTemplate Theme	**179**
Working with Template Variables	179
Variables Available in block.tpl.php	179
Variables Available in box.tpl.php	180
Variables Available in comment.tpl.php	181
Variables Available in node.tpl.php	181
Variables Available in page.tpl.php	182
Intercepting and Overriding Variables	184
Making New Variables Available	185
Dynamic Theming	185
Using Multiple Templates	186
Dynamically Theming Page Elements	189
Creating Dynamic CSS Styling	191
Build a New Pure PHP Theme	**193**
Required Elements	194
HTML Headers	196

Head of Document	196
Implementing the Features	196
Favicon	196
Logo	197
Site Name	197
Site Slogan	197
Primary and Secondary Links	198
Sidebars	198
Sidebar Left	198
Sidebar Right	199
Main Content Area	199
Title and Breadcrumb Trail	199
Tabs	199
Help	199
Messages	200
Content Region	200
Footer	200
Theme Closure	200
Overriding Functions	201
Summary	**201**
Chapter 8: Dealing with Forms	**203**
How Forms Work in Drupal	**203**
Modifying and Overriding Form Functions	**206**
Adding HTML via Function Attributes	207
Using form_alter()	207
Overriding Form Functions from template.php	209
Creating Custom Templates for Forms	211
Page Templates	211
Block Templates	212
Templates for Forms Output	213
Common Form Issues	**214**
Modifying Data Labels and Other Text	214
Using form_alter()	214
Override the Function	215
Create a New Template	215
Add a Node	215
Modifying the Styling of a Form	216
Using form_alter()	217
Override the Function	217
Create a New Template	217
Using Images for Buttons	217
The Default Forms	**218**
The User Forms	219
The Login Forms	219

The User Registration Form   220
The Request Password Form   221
The Edit User Info Form   222
The Default Contact Form   223
The Search Forms   224
The Theme Search Form   225
The Block Search Form   226
The Page Search Form   226
The Advanced Search Form   227
The Search Results Page   228
The Poll Module Forms   228
The Poll Block Form   229
The Poll Page Form   229
Summary   **229**
Appendix A   **231**
Index   **239**

Preface

This book sets out to explain the workings of the Drupal theme framework, and how you can use it effectively. The goal of this book is to explain basic principles, demonstrate practical solutions to common problems, and create a reference for theming.

The book begins with an overview of the theme system and an explanation of what is included in the default Drupal distro. We next look at how you can squeeze the most out of the default system. The middle chapters discuss PHPTemplate and introduce using themeable functions and manipulating the Drupal style sheets. To illustrate the principles, we take a common theme and modify it. In the final chapters, we delve into creating themes from scratch and more advanced issues, like forms.

For purposes of this text, we focus on the theme engine included in the default distro—PHPTemplate. Similarly, we only touch on creating themes in pure PHP, without the use of a theme engine.

This book is all about controlling the presentation layer of your Drupal site; accordingly, we do not cover creating new modules, or writing custom functionality.

The author of this text comes from a design background and has only basic programming skills. The explanations given, and the rational for many of the choices, reflect the author's background. In that light, this book may not always satisfy hardcore programmers who expect the technical issues to be explained in detail. It should, however, make the life of many designers a little easier and hopefully, with the reference materials we've included, find a lasting home on the shelves of many Drupal developers.

What This Book Covers

Chapter 1 covers the elements of a Drupal theme. It also takes a look at the contents of the Drupal distro and examines the different approaches of the default themes.

Chapter 2 explains how to set up and configure a theme in Drupal. By way of example, we take a default theme and customize it using only the options provided by the system.

Chapter 3 discusses the use of theme engines in general and the PHPTemplate engine in particular. This chapter also lays the groundwork for techniques to modify themes through the system's CSS and themeable functions.

Chapter 4 takes an in-depth look at the system's default style sheets and the various themeable functions.

Chapter 5 explains the process behind intercepting and overriding the Drupal style sheets and themeable functions. This is a key concept for obtaining full control over the presentation layer—without the necessity of modifying the core files.

Chapter 6 provides a hands-on example of the techniques covered in the previous chapters by taking a default theme and then modifying it extensively.

Chapter 7 covers creating a theme from scratch with the PHPTemplate theme engine and also looks at the basics of implementing a theme without a theme engine.

Chapter 8 discusses modifying the look and feel of the many different forms in the Drupal system.

Appendix A is a listing of all the selectors in the various style sheets.

What You Need for This Book

Throughout this book, we will assume that you have the following package installed and available:

- Drupal CMS (version 5.x)

Who is This Book for

The main requirements of this book are knowledge of HTML, CSS, and a touch of creativity! Though this book aims to make Drupal theming accessible to designers, theming in Drupal 5 involves writing some PHP code, and a basic knowledge of PHP will be helpful.

Conventions

In this book, you will find a number of styles of text that distinguish between different kinds of information. Here are some examples of these styles, and an explanation of their meaning.

There are three styles for code. Code words in text are shown as follows: "We can include other contexts through the use of the `include` directive."

A block of code will be set as follows:

```
title {
  color: #666;
  font-size: 1.8em;
  line-height: 2.0em;
  font-style: italic;
```

When we wish to draw your attention to a particular part of a code block, the relevant lines or items will be made bold:

```
<div id="block-<?php print $block->module .'-'. $block->delta; ?>"
class="clear-block block block-<?php print $block->module ?>">
<?php if ($block->subject): ?>
  <h2><?php print $block->subject ?></h2>
```

New terms and **important words** are introduced in a bold-type font. Words that you see on the screen, in menus or dialog boxes for example, appear in our text like this: "clicking the **Next** button moves you to the next screen".

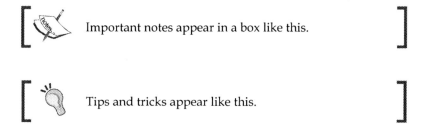

Important notes appear in a box like this.

Tips and tricks appear like this.

Reader Feedback

Feedback from our readers is always welcome. Let us know what you think about this book, what you liked or may have disliked. Reader feedback is important for us to develop titles that you really get the most out of.

To send us general feedback, simply drop an email to `feedback@packtpub.com`, making sure to mention the book title in the subject of your message.

If there is a book that you need and would like to see us publish, please send us a note in the **SUGGEST A TITLE** form on www.packtpub.com or email suggest@packtpub.com.

If there is a topic that you have expertise in and you are interested in either writing or contributing to a book, see our author guide on www.packtpub.com/authors.

Customer Support

Now that you are the proud owner of a Packt book, we have a number of things to help you to get the most from your purchase.

Downloading the Example Code for the Book

Visit http://www.packtpub.com/support, and select this book from the list of titles to download any example code or extra resources for this book. The files available for download will then be displayed.

 The downloadable files contain instructions on how to use them.

Errata

Although we have taken every care to ensure the accuracy of our contents, mistakes do happen. If you find a mistake in one of our books—maybe a mistake in text or code—we would be grateful if you would report this to us. By doing this you can save other readers from frustration, and help to improve subsequent versions of this book. If you find any errata, report them by visiting http://www.packtpub.com/support, selecting your book, clicking on the **Submit Errata** link, and entering the details of your errata. Once your errata are verified, your submission will be accepted and the errata added to the list of existing errata. The existing errata can be viewed by selecting your title from http://www.packtpub.com/support.

Questions

You can contact us at questions@packtpub.com if you are having a problem with some aspect of the book, and we will do our best to address it.

1
The Elements of a Drupal Theme

In this chapter, we will introduce themes and their role in the Drupal system. The chapter also covers the various types of themes, the basic elements of a theme, and the functions those elements fulfil. Near the end of the chapter, we will also look at the themes contained in the distro and examine exactly what it is that makes each theme distinct.

The contents of this preliminary chapter provide the general comprehension necessary to grasp the big picture of Drupal. Think of the knowledge communicated in this chapter as a framework from which we will hang the various skills that follow in the subsequent chapters.

What is a Theme?

In the context of Drupal, the term "theme" means a collection of files that are responsible for the look and feel of the website. Other systems use different names for the files that perform the same function in their particular systems—the most common term used elsewhere being "template."

Throughout, we will use "theme" to refer to the collection of files responsible for displaying the information on the page. We will use "template" to refer to certain specific elements of the theme, particularly in relation to the templating engine used in Drupal.

Conceptually, a theme is a visual container that is used to format and display data on the screen. Expressed in terms of its component parts, a theme is a collection of files that format data into the presentation layer viewed by site visitors and system administrators. Expressed in simplest terms: The theme determines how your site looks!

A theme will contain many files that are familiar to web designers, including typically, style sheets, images, and JavaScript. They are also likely to carry some files that may not be so familiar, for example ***.theme**, or ***.tpl.php files**. The former is used by pure PHP themes; the latter extension appears in themes that employ the PHPTemplate templating engine bundled with Drupal.

Official Drupal Online Resources

resource	URL
Main Drupal Site	`http://www.drupal.org`
Drupal Forums	`http://drupal.org/forum`
Download Extensions	`http://drupal.org/project`
Drupal Theming Handbook	`http://drupal.org/handbook/customization`

What is a Templating Engine?

A templating engine is a collection of scripts and files that serve to interpret the templating language and process the commands contained therein. As the data is produced from the database queries and from outside sources (if any), the template engine fulfills the function of plugging the data into a pre-determined format for display.

There exist a number of popular templating engines, each of which is designed to interpret different templating languages. Drupal is distributed with the PHPTemplate engine. PHPTemplate is popular for a variety of reasons, not the least of which is that the templating language it interprets is good old PHP—a preferred choice for many Web developers today.

While PHPTemplate is distributed with the Drupal core, there are a variety of other templating engines that can also be installed and used with the Drupal system. Among the most popular are XTemplate, Smarty, and PHPTal. These alternative templating engines can be downloaded from `http://drupal.org/project/Theme+engines`.

The Range and Flexibility of Drupal Themes

What can be done with a Drupal theme? How much presentation flexibility does the system have? These are key questions that arise when evaluating Drupal for your project. The themes included in the default distro, while useful, don't really offer much in the way of variety. But don't let the default themes prejudice your thinking too much; Drupal can be used to create a wide variety of layout styles, from traditional portal layouts to more cutting edge sites.

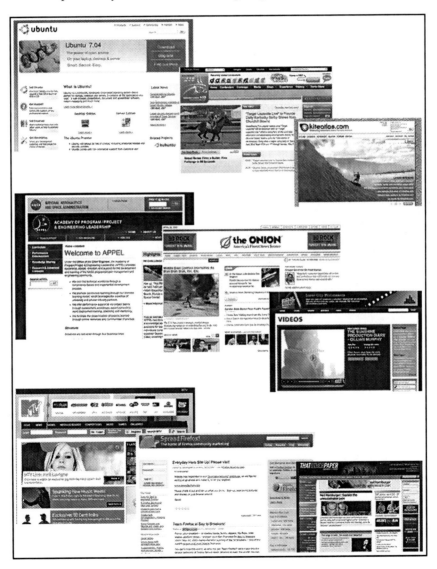

When assessing a CMS for flexibility, programmers and designers often look at the issue differently. Programmers tend to focus on the developmental potential the system offers with its range of available theme engines and the use of the popular PHP programming language. Designers, on the other hand, are typically more concerned with determining what restrictions a system imposes on their ability to design the interfaces desired by their clients.

There is good news for both parties. For programmers, the inclusion of the PHPTemplate engine in the Drupal distro means it is possible to tailor the output to match a variety of criteria. The system offers the ability to create custom templates and to specify your modified files over the default files—all without having to actually hack the Drupal core.

For designers, the flexibility of the Drupal approach to site building allows for the creation of attractive and brand-sensitive interfaces (not just a cookie-cutter portal or blog site).

While it may take a while for a new-comer to wade through the Drupal approach to the presentation layer, it is worth the effort, as a little knowledge can go a long way towards allowing you to tailor the system's output to your specific needs.

Who's using Drupal? Some big names…

NASA	`http://appel.nasa.gov/`
The Onion	`http://www.theonion.com`
MTV (UK)	`http://www.mtv.co.uk/`
Ubuntu	`http://www.ubuntu.com/`
Mozilla (Spread Firefox)	`http://www.spreadfirefox.com/`

What You See on the Screen

When you access a Drupal website, what you see on the screen is the result of the site's active theme files. As the theme files call the data, the files also set the styling, position, and placement of the content on your screen. A lot of work for a small group of files…

Within a web page layout, a Drupal theme designer will designate certain general areas to fulfill certain functions. For example, in a typical 3-column theme, the center is used to hold the primary content whereas the two smaller side columns contain secondary information. Screen space within each of those areas is also allocated according to the designer's priorities.

In Drupal, that main content area is often called the *content column* and those columns on the side are usually called *sidebars*.

Drupal theme files segregate the elements on the page through the definition of markers called *regions*. A theme developer can place the regions anywhere on the page by adding a short statement to the code of the appropriate file. Wherever regions have been specified, the site administrator can then assign module output, which in Drupal-speak is called a *block*.

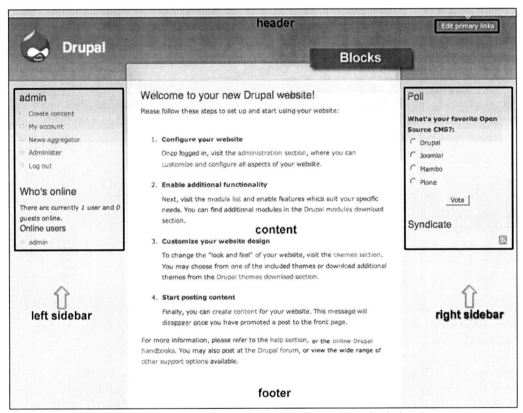

The default Garland theme, showing hard-coded Regions and sample Block assignments. Note how the Blocks are nested inside specific Regions

Regions are, in other words, placeholders inside the page layout into which a site administrator can position functional output; this is most frequently done by assigning blocks to the region desired.

Regions must be coded into your theme files and are, therefore, primarily the province of the theme developer. Blocks, on the other hand, can be created and manipulated by the site administrator (without having to modify the code).

Blocks can be created in two fashions: First, whenever the site administrator activates a module that produces visual output, a parallel block of the same name automatically becomes active. The administrator can then assign the block to where ever they want the module's output to appear. Alternatively, the administrator can manually create and display a new block from within the blocks manager.

Regions that have no content assigned to them are inactive, but remain eligible for block assignment. Note in the illustration that the regions labeled *header*, *left sidebar*, *right sidebar*, and *content* all have output assigned to them. Those regions are active. The footer region, in contrast, has no output assigned to it and is inactive on this particular page.

To view the block placement in each of the default templates of your distro, log in to your Drupal site as an administrator and then go to **administer>site building>blocks**. Click each of the themes' names to view the block placement, which will be overlaid on your screen.

The Big Picture: How Drupal Displays a Page

In order to appreciate fully the philosophy behind theming and the rationale behind the approach to modifying and creating themes that is presented in this text, it is useful to see how Drupal functions at run time.

The shortest explanation of how a CMS functions can be expressed as follows: Text and pointers to other kinds of content are stored in the database; that data is then dynamically retrieved, composed, and presented to a user in response to a request sent from a web browser. Drupal functions in the same manner, with the themes playing the crucial role in the formatting and presentation of the contents.

To illustrate the topic in more detail, consider the following:

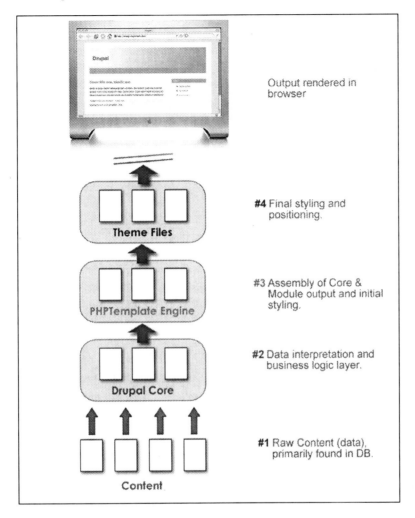

The diagram shows a hierarchy, wherein the lowest level is the raw data and the highest level is the final output displayed on the page. The diagram also shows an order of precedence in which the items at the top of the hierarchy, nearest the browser, take precedence over items lower in the order.

By way of further explanation:

1. The data, for the most part, is stored in basic form in the database of your installation. Formatting, if any, is present only as HTML tags that may have been specified in the content by the author.

2. The first significant step on the way to output occurs when the Drupal core extracts and pre-processes the data. No real formatting occurs at this level. Any HTML formatting specified in items stored in the DB is simply passed through for interpretation by the browser.

3. The next step on the way to output sees the templating engine begin to assemble to core and module output into something close to final form.

4. The final step prior to output occurs when the theme-specific files process the data. This last stage can have a wide range of impacts, from minimal to very significant. The variance in impact depends on the extent to which the theme's author has provided specific directions for the formatting of various items and whether the author has chosen to override the formatting of the templating engine or of the default style sheets in the Drupal distro—all topics we will cover in depth later in this book.

The Importance of Themes in Drupal

The role of themes in the Drupal system relates to the presentation layer of a website, that is, what the site visitors and administrators experience through their browsers. The files in a theme provide HTML formatting, CSS styling, and additional logic that frames the output of the system's functionality. All of these elements come together to create what the site visitor sees in their web browser.

While the default Drupal distro includes a set of themes which will be sufficient for many users, I assume you are reading this book out of a desire to do more, whether it be only to install additional themes and then modify them to suit your needs, or whether you plan to build your own themes from scratch.

In order to grasp better some of the challenges (and opportunities) associated with the Drupal themes, it is useful to look at three key concepts that impact the way you use the system and the way in which you must plan your theme deployment.

Key Concepts

We're going to look next at three key concepts relating to Drupal themes. Those three concepts are:

1. You Can Theme It All
2. Build with Blocks
3. Intercept and Override

You Can Theme It All

One source of confusion for many new users of Drupal is the fact that the default administrator interface is the same as the front-end interface seen by site visitors. Unlike other content management systems, there is not a purpose-built administration interface in Drupal.

During the installation process, the system is configured to display the Garland template for both the front end and the back end. This is yet another example of the high level of integration typical to Drupal. If you want to work with one consistent template throughout, you can.

The seamless integration of the administrator interface into the site works well in some cases, but in others it may be problematic. There will be situations where the use of the same theme for the visitors and the administrators is undesirable, for example, on a marketing-oriented site where the artistic theme used for the site visitors may be impractical for site administrators.

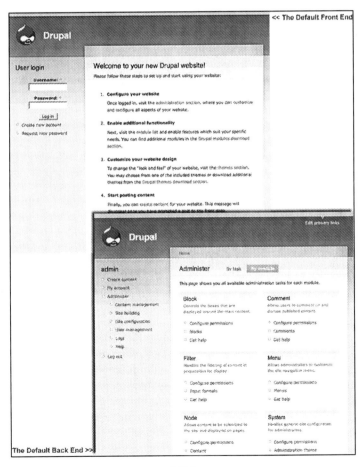

The system's default use of the same page template for both the front end and the back end conceals the existence of a great deal of flexibility and makes it non-obvious that you can do more with the themes. That's the bad news. The good news is that you can do more—much more!

The Drupal system allows you to specify different page templates for different purposes on your site. You can, for example, build one page template for your home page, another for your interior pages, and yet another for your administrator's use. The sky is the limit on this point as the templating engine also gives you the ability to provide a variety of styling for very specific types of contents or for the output of a particular module. The control is highly granular and with a little practice (and a little ingenuity) you will find the system to be very flexible indeed.

In the following chapters, we will look at how to implement multiple themes and how to theme and configure all the various constituent parts of the Drupal system. You can theme it all!

Build with Blocks

As noted earlier in this chapter, the code of a Drupal theme includes placeholders called regions. The regions are areas in a page where content will be displayed. The site administrator can then assign a variety of output to the regions through the admin interface.

One of the most common sources of output is the Drupal modules. Modules are stand-alone bits of code—mini applications in some cases—that extend the functionality of your site. The default distro includes a large number of modules. It is through modules that Drupal provides functions like the Forum, the Aggregator and even additional administrative power, like the Throttle module.

Some modules produce output that appears on the screen, for example, the Forum module produces a threaded discussions functionality with extensive output. Other modules simply add functionality, for example the Ping module, which notifies other sites when your content has changed. The administrator is able to toggle modules on or off and able to assign the output of those modules—called blocks—to the various regions in the theme.

The process of activating modules and assigning blocks to regions on the pages is one of the most basic and most important skills for a site administrator. Understanding how to administer the system and what options are available is key to building interesting and usable sites. A great deal of flexibility can be squeezed out of the system in this area alone.

This system, however, is not without complications. Module developers typically build their modules to be self-contained units. This independence also extends to the presentation layer of these discreet items of code. As a result, almost all the modules have distinct formatting and specific files that control that formatting. This approach to programming and modularization leads to a system in which a significant number of discrete units must be dealt with, adding greatly to the potential for complexity in changing the look and feel of a site to your specifications.

Core - optional

Enabled	Name	Version	Description
☐	Aggregator	5.1	Aggregates syndicated content (RSS, RDF, and Atom feeds).
☐	Blog	5.1	Enables keeping easily and regularly updated user web pages or blogs.
☐	Blog API	5.1	Allows users to post content using applications that support XML-RPC blog APIs.
☐	Book	5.1	Allows users to collaboratively author a book.
☑	Color	5.1	Allows the user to change the color scheme of certain themes.
☑	Comment	5.1	Allows users to comment on and discuss published content. Required by: Forum (disabled)
☐	Contact	5.1	Enables the use of both personal and site-wide contact forms.
☐	Drupal	5.1	Lets you register your site with a central server and improve ranking of Drupal projects by posting information on your installed modules and themes
☐	Forum	5.1	Enables threaded discussions about general topics. Depends on: Taxonomy (enabled), Comment (enabled)
☑	Help	5.1	Manages the display of online help.
☐	Legacy	5.1	Provides legacy handlers for upgrades from older Drupal installations.
☐	Locale	5.1	Enables the translation of the user interface to languages other than English.
☑	Menu	5.1	Allows administrators to customize the site navigation menu.
☐	Path	5.1	Allows users to rename URLs.
☐	Ping	5.1	Alerts other sites when your site has been updated.
☐	Poll	5.1	Allows your site to capture votes on different topics in the form of multiple choice questions.
☐	Profile	5.1	Supports configurable user profiles.
☐	Search	5.1	Enables site-wide keyword searching.
☐	Statistics	5.1	Logs access statistics for your site.
☑	Taxonomy	5.1	Enables the categorization of content. Required by: Forum (disabled)
☐	Throttle	5.1	Handles the auto-throttling mechanism, to control site congestion.
☐	Tracker	5.1	Enables tracking of recent posts for users.
☐	Upload	5.1	Allows users to upload and attach files to content.

The list of default modules available in Drupal

Each of the functional units above—each module—is kept in a separate directory inside the `Modules` folder. Many contain their own CSS files, creating a large number of style sheets scattered throughout the system. Add to that already daunting collection of modules any additional extensions you wish to install on your particular site and you can see how CSS juggling might come to dominate your life. Nevertheless, fear not, as styling all of this is manageable, using the technique discussed below.

In addition to the blocks produced by modules, you can also create blocks specific to your installation. Manually created blocks provide an easy avenue for placement of additional information (e.g., text or images), or, by inclusion of PHP code in the block, additional functionality.

Each of the blocks in the system, whether created by modules or manually created by the system administrator, can be themed individually, if you so desire.

Intercept and Override

The process of getting data from its raw form to its final displayed form provides several opportunities for you to affect the output prior to the data's arrival on the viewer's screen. While it is possible to work at the lower levels—hacking the core or the modules or the templating engine—I advise against that. The recognized best practice approach to customizing themes emphasizes making changes at the higher levels, primarily to the theme files themselves.

The best practice approach to customizing themes involves intercepting and overriding files and styles—not altering the core. In short, if you wish to style a particular block, instead of hacking the module that produces it, you will override the default module file with one of your own, or you will intercept the styles or functions of the module with your own; most likely, you will use a combination of both those techniques. The new files and styles you create will be part of the theme itself.

By choosing to affect the system's output at the highest levels of Drupal's processes, we leave the core in a purer state. This approach has several advantages, the most significant being that system upgrades and patches can be applied without fear of losing modifications necessary to your presentation. Sites customized in this manner are easier to maintain and your code remains portable and available for re-use in other deployments.

"override"—as used in this context, refers to creating a file, function, or style which is redundant with an existing file, function, or style and, courtesy of the order of precedence inherent in Drupal, the new file, function, or style will control.

The Contents of the Drupal Distro

The default distribution of Drupal comes with a variety of themes ready for use. The themes provide a basic variety in look and style and also serve an important didactic purpose, that is, helping those new to Drupal understand how themes work. By studying the themes in the distro, you can learn from functional examples how various theming techniques can be implemented successfully.

To view the various themes, login as an administrator, then go to **administer>themes**. This is the theme administration page and on this page you will see a list of the themes installed and the controls that allow you to enable, activate, and configure each of the themes.

There are six themes in the default distro:

- Bluemarine
- Chameleon
- Garland
- Marvin
- Minnelli
- Pushbutton.

The templates provide some variety in layout, options, colors, and accessibility. Four of the themes employ the PHPTemplate engine; two do not. The default theme which is automatically selected during the installation process is Garland. You can switch to any of the other templates easily from within the administration interface.

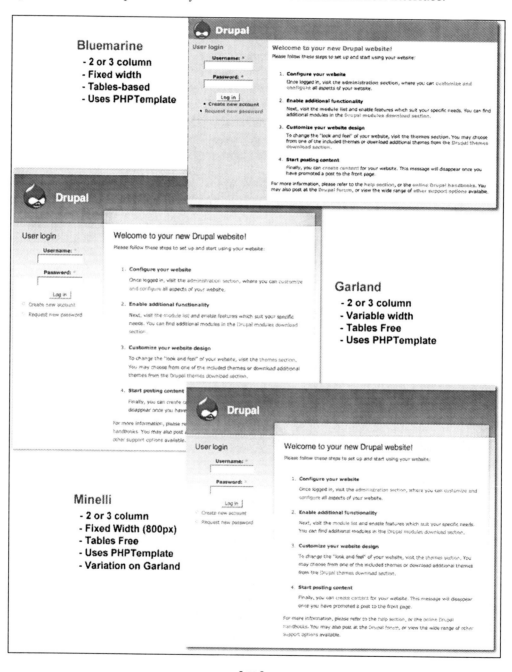

drupal

User login

Username: *

Password: *

Log in
- Create new account
- Request new password

Welcome to your new Drupal website!
Please follow these steps to set up and start using your website:

1. **Configure your website**

   Once logged in, visit the administration section, where you can customize and configure all aspects of your website.

2. **Enable additional functionality**

   Next, visit the module list and enable features which suit your specific needs. You can find additional modules in the Drupal modules download section.

3. **Customize your website design**

   To change the "look and feel" of your website, visit the themes section. You may choose from one of the included themes or download additional themes from the Drupal themes download section.

Chameleon

- 2 or 3 column
- Fixed width
- CSS-based
- Does not use PHPTemplate

Marvin

- 2 or 3 column
- Variable width
- CSS-based
- Does not use PHPTemplate
- Variation on Chameleon

 drupal

User login

Username: *

Password: *

Log in
- Create new account
- Request new password

Welcome to your new Drupal website!
Please follow these steps to set up and start using your website:

1. **Configure your website**

   Once logged in, visit the administration section, where you can customize and configure all aspects of your website.

2. **Enable additional functionality**

   Next, visit the module list and enable features which suit your specific needs. You can find additional modules in the Drupal modules download section.

3. **Customize your website design**

   To change the "look and feel" of your website, visit the themes section. You may choose from one of the included themes or download additional themes from the Drupal themes download section.

 Drupal

 User login

Username: *

Password: *

Log in
- Create new account
- Request new password

Welcome to your new Drupal website!
Please follow these steps to set up and start using your website:

1. **Configure your website**

   Once logged in, visit the administration section, where you can customize and configure all aspects of your website.

2. **Enable additional functionality**

   Next, visit the module list and enable features which suit your specific needs. You can find additional modules in the Drupal modules download section.

3. **Customize your website design**

   To change the "look and feel" of your website, visit the themes section. You may choose from one of the included themes or download additional themes from the Drupal themes download section.

Pushbutton

- 2 or 3 column
- Variable width
- Tables-based
- Uses PHPTemplate

To change templates, simply access **administrator>themes** in the admin interface and click the **Enabled** checkbox next to the theme you wish to activate. Select the radio button control marked **Default** if you wish to set the theme as the default. (The default theme will appear on all pages, which are not specifically assigned to another theme.) The new theme will automatically appear once your choice has been saved.

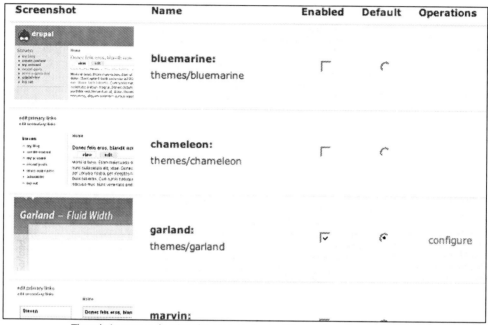

The admin screen showing the controls for enabling and configuring themes

All six templates contained in the distro can support either two or three column layouts, though in the default configuration you will see only two columns. The way in which these themes are designed creates the flexibility in the layout. The site administrator can assign items to a third column if desired; the third column will only appear when items are assigned to that position. When items are not assigned to the third column, the theme automatically collapses the unused region to show only two columns. The assignment of items to those columns is discussed in the next chapter.

The themes also vary in their approach to accessibility issues. Pushbutton and Bluemarine both employ tables in their layout. The other templates depend entirely upon CSS to place and control the elements on the page. (Table-based layouts are generally not preferred due to the barriers they erect to achieving accessible web pages.)

Note that two of the Themes, Minnelli and Marvin, are actually simple variations on other themes (specifically, Garland and Chameleon, respectively). The derivative themes are built on the same frameworks as their parents (note the visual similarity in the accompanying illustration), but employ different style sheets and use CSS to impart a different layout and a slightly different look. The presence of a dedicated `style.css` file in a subdirectory tells PHPTemplate to treat this as a separate theme, distinct from its parent.

The Theme Files

The themes and their respective files are kept in the directory named **themes** on your server. The default distro also comes bundled with the PHPTemplate engine. The PHPTemplate files are located in a sub-directory inside the **themes** directory on your server.

To view the theme and template engine files in your Drupal installation, access your server and navigate to the directory located at /themes.

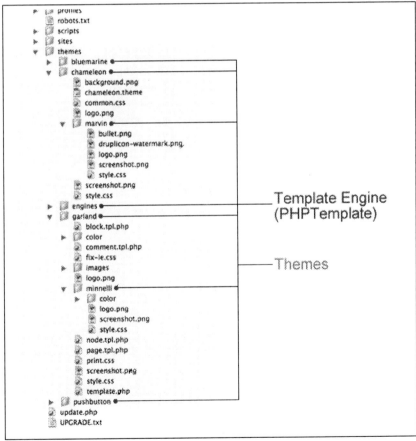

Screenshot of section of the default Drupal directory structure on a server

The sample templates included in the distro demonstrate the two principal methods of creating themes. The themes Bluemarine, Garland, Minnelli, and Pushbutton all employ the PHPTemplate engine. The themes Chameleon and Marvin are built without use of PHPTemplate. Both Chameleon and Marvin are written directly in PHP; themes that use this approach are sometimes referred to as "Pure" PHP themes.

Which approach is better for you? Hard to say; the answer will vary from person to person and according to your intended use. The right answer will depend largely on your needs and your relative skill with the technologies. (Building a pure PHP theme can be a challenge for those who lack strong PHP skills!) Speaking generally, the PHPTemplate approach is preferable as it is not only easier to master, but it is also more modular and reusable than a pure PHP approach to themes.

The Files of a PHPTemplate Theme

Let's look at the files that comprise the Bluemarine theme and their roles at run time:

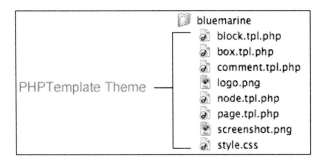

- `block.tpl.php` – Defines the appearance of the blocks on the page.
- `box.tpl.php` – Defines a specific format—a box used to frame things (like comments in the Bluemarine theme).
- `comment.tpl.php` – Defines the appearance of the comments which follow items.
- `logo.png` – An image file containing the logo used in the theme.
- `node.tpl.php` – Defines the appearance of the nodes.
- `page.tpl.php` – This is the primary theme file. This is the only required file in a PHPTemplate theme and typically defines the appearance of most of the page.
- `screenshot.png` – An image file containing a screenshot of the theme; this is used as a reference.
- `style.css` – The style sheet for this theme.

Note that not all of these files are necessary for a PHPTemplate theme to function properly. The two key files are `page.tpl.php` and `style.css`.

 While it is not necessary for the theme to function, it is best practice to always include `screenshot.png`, as this file is used in the admin interface to provide site administrators with a preview of the installed themes.

The file `page.tpl.php` does the heavy lifting in all PHPTemplate themes. This file is the only required file and it handles most of the styling as well as incorporating by reference any theme-specific overrides contained in related files. In the case of the Bluemarine theme, those additional overrides are:

- `block.tpl.php`
- `box.tpl.php`
- `comment.tpl.php`
- `node.tpl.php`

Overrides are not required—the overrides in the Bluemarine theme represent a decision made by the author of the theme to style specific elements. As this is within the discretion of the theme developer, the presence and extent of overrides will vary from theme to theme.

The PHPTemplate-specific files all follow the same naming convention ***.tpl.php**. The prefix of each of those files is specific in that they are intended to override functions defined elsewhere. For the system to recognize that these files in the theme directory are intended to override the originals, the names must be consistent with the originals. The naming of some of the other theme files is flexible and within the discretion of the author.

We will take an in depth look at the various PHPTemplate files and the concepts and rules relating to overrides in later chapters.

The Files of a Pure PHP Theme

Let's look at the files that comprise the Chameleon theme and their roles at run time.

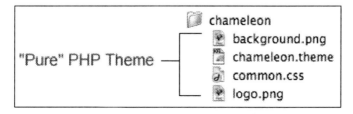

- `background.png` – An image file used as this theme's background.
- `chameleon.theme` – This is the primary theme file. This is the only required file in a pure PHP theme and it defines the appearance of the page.
- `common.css` – The style sheet for this theme.
- `logo.png` – An image file containing the logo used in the theme.

In this theme, the key pair of files is `chameleon.theme` and `common.css`. The `*.theme` file uses PHP to style page elements by overriding the default theme functions created by the system. The `*.css` contains the styles necessary to support the presentation.

We will take a more in depth look at pure PHP themes in later chapters.

Summary

This chapter lays the groundwork for what comes ahead. You should now have some familiarity with the big picture—with the basic terminology used in Drupal, with the way Drupal presents data at runtime, with the general functions of themes, templating engines and style sheets, and with the location and nature of the key files and directories.

You should also be aware that despite the apparent complexity one sees at first glance, that Drupal themes can be managed in a logical and relatively easy fashion by applying a strategy of intercepting and overriding the theme files.

2

Theme Set Up and Configuration

The large and active community of developers that has formed around Drupal guarantees a steady flow of themes for this popular CMS. The diversity of that community also assures that there will be a wide variety of themes produced. Add into the equation the existence of a growing number of commercial and open source web designs and you can be certain that somewhere out there is a design that is close to what you want. The issue becomes identifying the sources of themes and designs, and determining how much work you want to do yourself.

You can find both design ideas and complete themes on the Web. You need to decide whether you want to work with an existing theme, or convert a design into a theme, or whether you want to start from scratch, unburdened by any preliminary constraints or alien code. For purposes of this chapter, we will be dealing with finding, installing, and configuring an existing and current Drupal theme. In later chapters, we will look at converting designs and at building themes from scratch.

Near the end of this chapter, we take a default theme and run it through the entire customization process to see how far we can go with only the default resources at our disposal.

This chapter assumes you have a working Drupal installation, and that you have access to the files on your server.

Finding Additional Themes

There are several factors to consider when determining the suitability of an existing theme.

The first issue is compatibility. Due to changes made to Drupal in the 5.x series, older themes will not work properly with Drupal 5.x. Accordingly, your first step is to determine which version of Drupal you are running.

To find the version information for your installation, go to **Administer | Logs | Status Report**. The first line of the Status Report tabular data will show your version number.

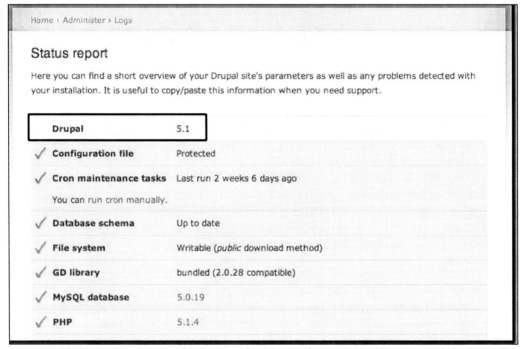

The Status Report screen showing Drupal version number. Note also this screen includes other useful information, like your MySQL and PHP version numbers

 If you do not see the Status Report option, then you are probably using a Drupal version earlier than 5.x. We suggest you upgrade as this book is for Drupal 5.x.

If you know your Drupal version, you can confirm whether the theme you are considering is usable on your system. If the theme you are looking at doesn't provide versioning information, assume the worst and make sure you back up your site before you install the questionable theme.

Once you're past the compatibility hurdle, your next concern is system requirements; does the theme require any additional extensions to work properly?

Some themes are ready to run with no additional extensions required. Many themes require that your Drupal installation include a particular templating engine. The most commonly required templating engine is PHPTemplate. If you are running a recent instance of Drupal, you will find that the PHPTemplate engine is installed by default. You can also download a variety of other popular templating engines, including Smarty and PHPTal from `http://drupal.org/project/Theme+engines`. Check carefully whether the theme you've chosen requires you to download and install other extensions. If so, track down the additional extensions and install them first, before you install your theme.

A good place to start looking for a complete Drupal theme is, perhaps not surprisingly, the official Drupal site. At Drupal.org, you can find a variety of downloads, including both themes and template engines. Go to `http://drupal.org/project/Themes` to find a listing of the current collection of themes. All the themes state very clearly the version compatibility and whether there are any prerequisites to run the theme.

In addition to the resources on the official Drupal site, there is an assortment of fan sites providing themes. Some sites are open source, others commercial, and a fair number are running unusual licenses (most frequently asking that footers be left intact with links back to their sites). Some of the themes available are great; most are average. If your firm is brand sensitive, or your design idiosyncratic, you will probably find yourself working from scratch.

Regardless of your particular needs, the theme repositories are a good place to start gathering ideas. Even if you cannot find exactly what you need, you sometimes find something with which you can work. An existing set of properly formed theme files can jump start your efforts and save you a ton of time.

If you wish to use an existing theme, pay attention to the terms of usage. You can save yourself (or your clients) major headaches by catching any unusual licensing provisions early in the process. There's nothing worse than spending hours on a theme only to discover its use is somehow restricted.

One source for designs with livable usage policies is the Open Source Web Design site, `http://www.oswd.org`, which includes a repository of designs, all governed by open source licensing terms. The down side of this resource is that all you get is the design—not the code, not a ready-made theme. You will need to convert the design into a usable theme.

For this chapter, let's search out a completed theme and for the sake of simplicity, let's take one from the official Drupal site. I am going to download the Gagarin theme from Drupal.org. I'll refer to this theme as a working example of some of the steps below. You can either grab a copy of the same theme or you can use another — the principles are the same regardless.

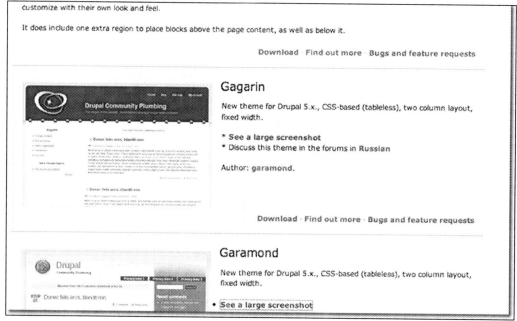

I downloaded Gagarin from `http://drupal.org/project/Themes`

Gagarin is an elegant little theme from Garamond of the Russian Drupal community. Gagarin is set up for a two-column site (though it can be run in three columns) and works particularly well for a blog site.

Installing an Additional Theme

Theme installation requires that you have the ability to move files from your local machine on to your server. Typically, this is done with an FTP client or through your hosting control panel file manager. The method you use is up to you, both have their advantages. It makes no difference to Drupal which method you choose to employ.

Odds are your theme was delivered to you as a single file containing a compressed archive of files. When I downloaded Gagarin, above, I wound up with the file `gagarin-5.x-1.x-dev.tar.gz`. The .tar.gz format (a.k.a. "tarball") is one of several commonly used to create compressed archives.

The first step towards getting the theme installed is to locally uncompress the archive. Double click the tarball and one of two things will happen: Either the file will uncompress and leave you with a new folder name "gagarin" or your system will prompt you to look for an application to open this file type. In the latter case, you will need to track down and install a file compression program. There are lots of good ones out there. Most users, however, should have no problems as compression software is installed on many systems these days.

Once you have successfully extracted the files, take a look at what you have. If there is a README file, read it now.

The next step is to get the extracted files up to your server. Use whatever means you prefer (FTP, control panel, etc.) to gain access to the directories of your Drupal site on the server.

Once you have access to your sever, navigate to the directory **sites/all**; this is where you will place all new theme files.

A note for old Drupal hands: The use of the **sites/all** directory is a change that was implemented in the version 5.x family. Using the **sites/all** directory instead of the traditional **themes** directory, allows you to run multiple sites off a single Drupal installation. Placing all your extensions inside the **sites/all** directory means less complication with future upgrades.

Next, in the **sites/all** directory, create a new sub-directory and name it **themes**. This new **themes** directory is where you will place all additional theme files. Finally, copy the **gagarin** directory and its contents inside **sites/all/themes**. Each theme should be kept in a separate directory. In this case you should have wound up with a directory structure like this: **sites/all/themes/gagarin**.

install.php	Jan 10, 2007, 6:15 PM	24 KB	PHP: Hypertext Pr...or (PHP) document
INSTALL.txt	Jan 8, 2007, 7:59 PM	12 KB	Plain text document
LICENSE.txt	Jul 9, 2006, 7:33 PM	20 KB	Plain text document
MAINTAINERS.txt	Dec 12, 2006, 1:09 AM	4 KB	Plain text document
misc	Jan 30, 2007, 8:20 AM	--	Folder
modules	Jan 30, 2007, 8:20 AM	--	Folder
profiles	Jan 30, 2007, 8:20 AM	--	Folder
robots.txt	Jan 8, 2007, 8:02 PM	4 KB	Plain text document
scripts	Jan 30, 2007, 8:20 AM	--	Folder
sites	Today, 10:24 PM	--	Folder
all	Today, 10:25 PM	--	Folder
README.txt	Dec 23, 2006, 11:35 PM	4 KB	Plain text document
themes	Today, 10:25 PM	--	Folder
gagarin	Today, 7:52 PM	--	Folder
default	Jan 30, 2007, 8:20 AM	--	Folder
themes	Today, 10:25 PM	--	Folder
update.php	Dec 26, 2006, 5:22 AM	32 KB	PHP: Hypertext Pr...or (PHP) document
UPGRADE.txt	Jan 9, 2007, 5:16 PM	4 KB	Plain text document
xmlrpc.php	Dec 11, 2005, 3:26 AM	4 KB	PHP: Hypertext Pr...or (PHP) document

Create the **sites/all/themes** directory to store the Gagarin theme files.

If all has gone according to plan, you are now ready to close your connection to your server and visit the admin interface of your Drupal site.

For the next steps, access the admin interface to your site via your browser. Navigate to **Administer|Site building|Themes**. You should see your new theme listed alphabetically in the list of themes, as per the illustration, below.

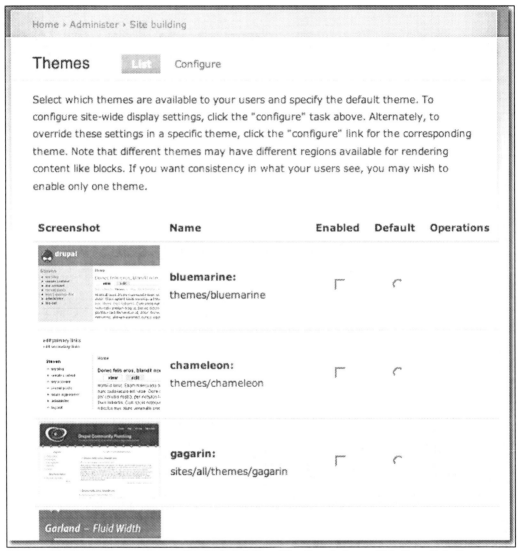

The Drupal theme manager after the installation of the Gagarin theme. Note the path to the theme files appears underneath each theme's name

The theme management screen presents you with a list of all the themes available on your site. Note the **Enabled** checkbox and the **Default** radio button; these controls are key to making a theme display on the site.

To set up Gagarin, first we must enable it, then assign it to appear where we want, then configure it.

To enable Gagarin, select the **Enabled** checkbox to the right of the theme name. In Drupal, you must enable each theme you wish to use on the site.

Once you've selected **Enable**, then click the **Save Configuration** button at the bottom of the screen. Note that the appearance of the site does not change—that is because the new theme is neither assigned to any pages (nodes) nor is it set as the default.

Next, let's assign the theme to appear where we want. In this case, I want Gagarin to appear throughout the site, so I am going to select the **Default** radio button. The **Default** control is important; it sets the primary theme—the default theme—for the site. The default theme will be used by the system in all situations in which another theme is not specified. If we click the **Default** radio button next to our new theme and click **Save Configuration**, the theme will be applied immediately, for both front end and back end of the site.

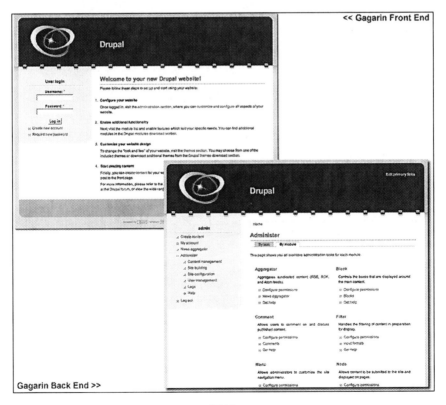

Note that you can enable more than one theme at a time. By enabling more than one theme, another function becomes possible. Registered visitors can choose which theme to use when they view the site. When multiple themes are enabled, a registered user can pick a theme as their default theme and the system will remember their choice.

When the multiple theme function is active, site visitors can select their preferred theme via the **Theme configuration** preferences on the **edit** tab of the **My account** page. This functionality can be disabled by the administrator.

Note that once you enable a theme, another choice appears on the Theme Manager interface. Enabling a theme causes the **Configure** option to become active (it will appear to the right of the **Default** radio button in the column labeled **Operations)**. The Configuration Manager provides access to both global configuration options and theme-specific settings. In the next section, we will take a look at both.

Configuring a Theme

In this section, we're going to go through the system and highlight the configuration options that are part of the default Drupal distro. We're not going to install any additional extensions or modify any code—we're going to focus exclusively on what can be done straight out of the box. We'll then apply this knowledge with an example configuration of the Garland default theme in the section that follows this one.

To begin, navigate to the theme manager (**Administer | Site building | Themes)**. Access the configuration options of the Garland theme by clicking the **configure** link in the right hand column.

The Garland theme as it appears in the Theme Manager. The configure link is in the right hand column

The Theme Configuration screen provides access to both global configuration and theme-specific configuration settings. As the name implies, global configuration is used to apply configuration choices consistently site wide—even across multiple themes. The theme specific configuration options relate only to a particular theme.

If there is a conflict between the theme specific configuration settings and the global configuration settings, the theme specific settings will take precedence.

Theme-Specific Configuration Options

The initial view on your screen is the theme-specific configuration options. In Garland, that looks like the following illustration:

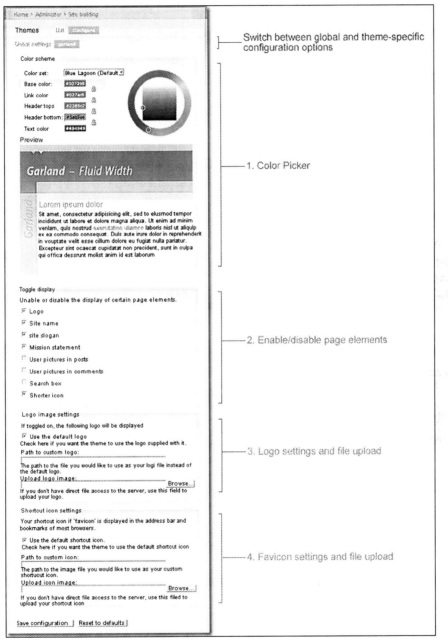

The Theme-specific configuration options available with the Garland theme

Let's break this down and look at what each section of the configuration manager can do.

Color Picker

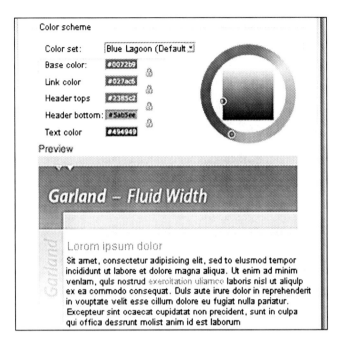

The Color Picker is a nifty little tool made possible by color.module, which is included by default in the core. Not all themes support this configuration option, but when they do, this is a dead easy way to modify the colors used throughout the theme. The best way to learn this tool is to just get in and play with it. It is a simple tool and the range of choices and the limitations become apparent pretty quickly.

 The padlock icons on the Color Picker color fields are used to lock in the relationship between two or more color choices. This allows you to experiment with different color combinations, all the while keeping the relationship between the various colors intact.

Enable/Disable Page Elements

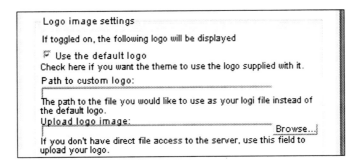

The Page Elements section contains a set of options that can be toggled on or off. Many of the options in this section relate to fundamental elements of the look and feel like the logo, site name, slogan, and mission statement. Other options are specific to certain types of functionality, for example, whether to show or hide the users' pictures in posts or comments. Note that two of the checkboxes in this section, **Logo** and **Shortcut icon**, affect the two sections that appear below. Note also that the **Search box** option that appears on this page is dependent on the Search module being active. If the Search module is disabled, the search box option will not be available.

 You can enable/disable the Search module from the Modules Manager, located at **Administer | Site building | Modules**.

Logo Settings

The Logo section allows you to select which logo the site theme will use. This section is dependent on the **Logo** checkbox being selected in the Page Elements section, above. If the **Logo** checkbox is selected, then the administrator has the choice between using the default logo included with the theme, or of providing an alternative logo. An upload option allows the administrator to upload a new logo image directly from the admin interface, without having to resort to another application. Once the logo is uploaded, note that the location and name the system has given to the logo file appears in the box labeled **Path to custom logo**.

Favicon Settings

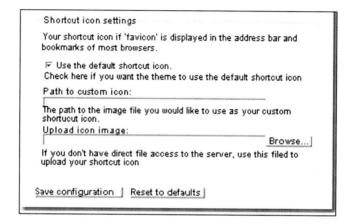

The Shortcut icon section allows you to select which favicon the site theme will use. Like the Logo section, this section is dependent on the **Shortcut icon** checkbox being selected in the Page Elements section, above. If the Shortcut icon checkbox is selected, then the administrator has the choice between using the default favicon included with the template, or of providing an alternative favicon. An upload option allows the administrator to upload a new favicon directly from the admin interface, without having to resort to another application. Once the favicon is uploaded, note that the location of the favicon file appears in the box labeled **Path to custom icon**.

The options discussed above are, as noted above, theme-specific. The options will vary from theme to theme, depending on the choices made by the theme developer when they created the theme. Compare for example, the options available in the Garland theme with those in the Chameleon and Marvin themes.

Global Configuration Settings

In addition to the theme-specific configuration options, the administrator can also access and change the Global configuration settings by selecting the **Global** tab at the top of the Theme Configuration page.

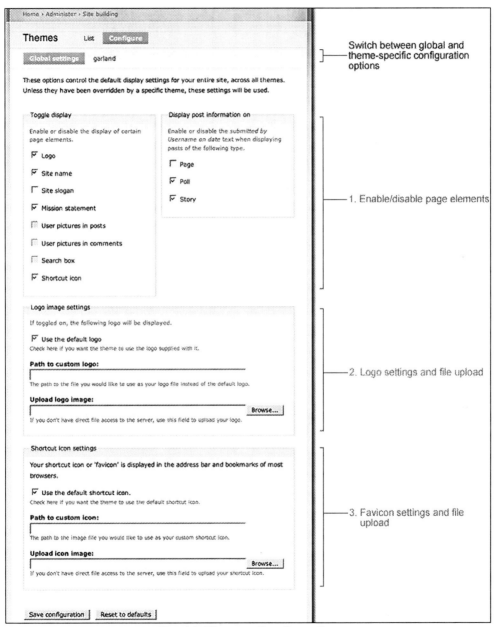

The global theme configuration options

You will note there is a great deal of similarity between the Global Configuration options and the Site Configuration options. The choices mean the same in both sections and operate in the same manner. The only difference is in the **Enable/Disable Page Elements** section where the **Display post information on** option appears.

The **Display post information on** option is unique to the Global Theme Configuration manager. The three controls in this box control allow you to select whether the text "**submitted by (Username) on (date)**" appears to viewers of certain types of content.

Managing Modules and Blocks

Modules are plug-ins which extend the functionality of the Drupal core. The Modules you select to use and the positioning of their output (Blocks) on the page can affect greatly the look and feel of your site. Managing effectively the various Modules and Blocks is a key to controlling the user experience on your site.

The standard Drupal distro includes a number of modules, only some of which are active in the default configuration. You can enable additional modules or disable some of the optional ones to achieve the functionality you desire.

 A variety of modules can be found on the official Drupal site at
`http://drupal.org/project/Modules`

The Module Manager

The Module Manager (**Administer | Site building | Modules**) includes a list of all available installed Modules. The default modules are categorized as **Core – optional** and **Core – required**. As you add additional modules to your installation, other group names may appear.

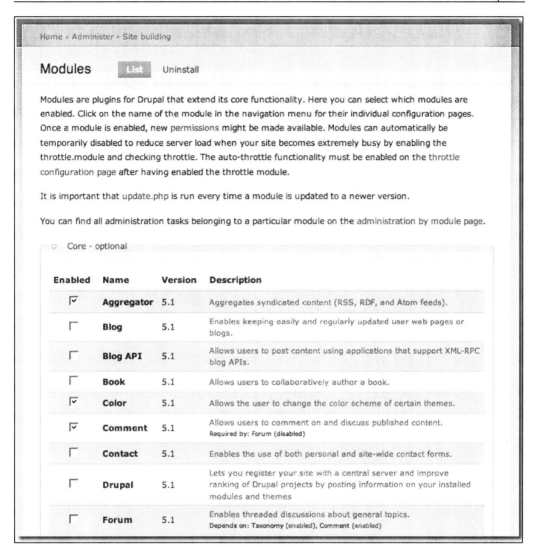

The Modules Manager

To enable a Module, simply access the Module Manager and then click the checkbox to the left of the Module's name. De-select the box to disable the Module. Once you have made your choices, click the **Save configuration** button at the bottom of the page.

Additional Modules can be downloaded and installed easily. Note that while you can disable any Module, you should not delete any of the Required Core Modules or else you will lose critical or important functionality on your site.

Enabling a new module may result in additional user permissions that need to be set, or other configuration decisions that need to be taken by the administrator. To access all the user permissions and configuration screens in one place, view your administrator console by module.

Blocks are output generated by the various components in the system. In many cases, enabling a Module automatically creates one or more related Blocks. Accordingly, your next step after enabling a Module should be a visit to the Blocks Manager.

The Blocks Manager

The tasks relating to Block management are accessed through the Blocks Manager, which can be found at **Administer | Site building | Blocks**.

The Blocks Manager interface looks like this:

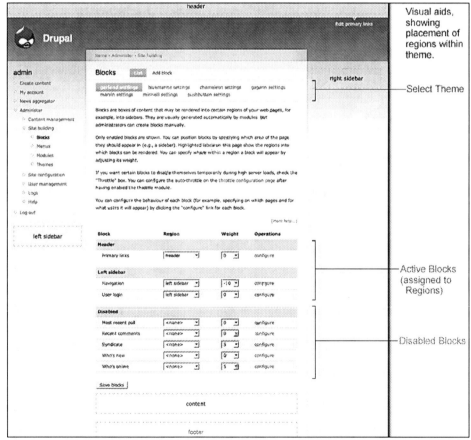

The Blocks Manager. Note that the system helps with Block assignment by showing all the active regions in the theme

The Blocks manager gives you control over a number of useful aspects relevant to your theme. First, and of primary importance is the ability to publish Blocks to Regions of your theme, thereby allowing you to position the output on the screen.

To assign a Block to a Region, select the target Region from the combo box immediately to the right of the Block's name. Click the **Save blocks** button. When the page reloads, the Block will have been moved to reflect the new assignment; if all things necessary for output to appear have been satisfied, the output will now also appear on the page.

For a Block to be visible, the Block must be both enabled and assigned to an active Region on the page.

Hiding a block is just as easy: Simply select **<none>** from the combo box and then click **Save blocks**; the Block will be immediately hidden from view.

 Remember that Region placement may vary from theme to theme. If you are using multiple themes on your site, be sensitive to Block placement across themes.

You can also manage the ordering of Blocks from the Blocks Manager. Immediately to the right of the Region combo box is the **Weight** combo box.

Weight, as the term is used in this context, reflects the ordering of Blocks within a single Region. A "lighter" Block will float up in the ordering, while a "heavier" Block will sink down relative to other Blocks. A weight of -1 is less than a weight of 1. Accordingly, the lightest setting is -10, the heaviest setting is 10. Don't forget to click the **Save configuration** button after you have chosen the weight of your Block.

Configuring Individual Blocks

The Blocks Manager also gives us access to the configuration options for each of our Blocks. Blocks can be configured at any time. Simply click the Block's **configure** link in the far right **Operations** column. Let's crack open the User Login Block and look at the configuration options presented there, as they are typical of the group.

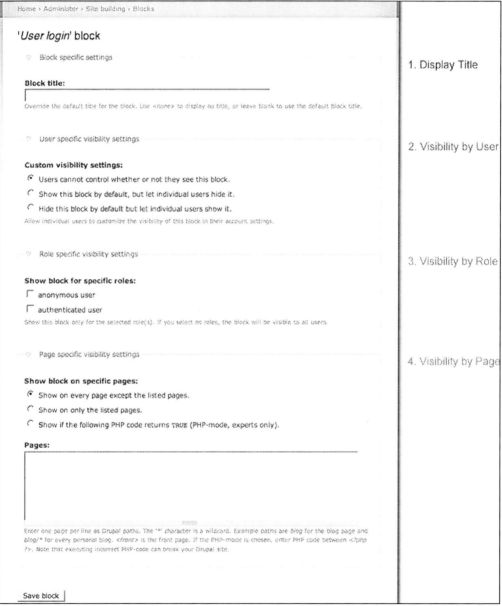

Configuring the User Login Block – a typical Block configuration screen

The Block configuration page provides options for naming and displaying the Block. All parameters on this page are optional.

Block Title

The first option, **Block title**, gives you a free text field into which you can enter a specific name that will override the default Block name. If nothing is entered, the default name (supplied by the system for the default blocks) will appear. If you wish no title to appear with the Block, then enter <none> in the text field provided.

The remaining options all relate to the visibility of the block. You are able to control when the block will appear to a user by setting and applying the conditions on this screen.

User Specific Visibility Settings

The first option, labeled **User specific visibility settings**, allows you to give users the freedom to show or hide blocks and to set their own preferences regarding whether the block displays by default. If you do not wish to grant users this discretion, leave the default setting.

Role Specific Visibility Settings

The second option is labeled **Role specific visibility setting**. The system presents you with 2 boxes, but 3 choices. If you want everyone to see the block, leave the default state. Alternatively, you can show the block only to authenticated users (i.e., users who have logged in) or only to anonymous users (i.e., users who have not logged in).

In addition to the parameters on this page, blocks can also be hidden during busy periods to decrease load on your server. The throttle module controls this specialized visibility setting.

Page Specific Visibility Settings

The final option is labeled **Page specific visibility settings**, but the label is actually a bit of a misnomer, as you can do much more here than simply tie block visibility to the page on the screen. The first two options allow you to list pages to include, or exclude, the display of the block. To enable this function, select the appropriate radio button then enter the URLs of the pages you wish to specify in the box below.

Let's look at the syntax for this window, as the Drupal system requires you to specify things in a particular fashion. Note that there are also some good shortcuts available here which will save you from having to enter a number of URLs to capture every single page of a particular content area or functionality:

term	designates
<front>	The home page
admin	The Admin main page
admin/*	All URLs that include admin/
aggregator/*	The RSS Aggregator main page
aggregator/x	The RSS Aggregator with the ID of x (where x is an integer)
aggregator	All URLs that include aggregator/
blog	The blog main page
blog/x	The blog with the ID of x (where x is an integer)
blog/*	All URLS that include blog/ (every personal blog main page)
contact	The default system Contact form
forum	The Forum main page
forum/x	The Forum with the ID of x (where x is an integer)
forum/*	All URLs that include forum/ (every forum main page)
node/x	An item with the node ID of x (where x is an integer)
user/*	The User pages.
user/x	The main page of the user with the ID of x (where x is an integer)

Note that you can use more than one statement at a time. To use multiple statements, simply input them on separate lines in the text box. One consideration to keep in mind is that you cannot specify at the same time, pages on which a Block will appear as well as pages on which the Block does not appear—those options are mutually exclusive.

The third radio button on this section is where the fun begins (and this should arguably be a separate control on the page, but the Drupal team simplified the interface by just listing it all under one section). If you select the third button, then you are able to enter PHP code that can control the visibility of the block in almost literally any fashion you choose. Don't be fooled by the label they put on it—**Pages**—this is a wild card field in which you can apply PHP code that can be used to establish logic that determines visibility according to various criteria.

Adding PHP to Blocks

With PHP statements Blocks management becomes much more interesting. You can add custom visibility settings of any variety. Tie visibility to a user, to a role, to a content type or whatever combination is needed for your site.

Let's look at some examples:

1. Display a Block only to the user who's User ID = 1:

```php
<?php
global $user;
if ($user->uid == 1){
  return TRUE;
}
else {
  return FALSE;
}
?>
```

2. Display a Block only to users who belong to a particular role (in this example, the role = Moderator):

```php
<?php
global $user;
if (in_array('Moderator',$user->roles)) {
  return TRUE;
}
else {
  return FALSE;
}
?>
```

3. Display a Block only for a specific content type (in this example, the content type = story):

```php
<?php
$match = FALSE;
$types = array('story' => 1);
if (arg(0) == 'node' && is_numeric(arg(1))) {
  $nid = arg(1);
  $node = node_load(array('nid' => $nid));
  $type = $node->type;
  if (isset($types[$type])) {
    $match = TRUE;
  }
}
return $match;
?>
```

4. Display a Block throughout all Forums:

```php
<?php
if (arg(0) == 'forum') {
  return TRUE;
}
if (arg(0) == 'node' && ctype_digit(arg(1))) {
  $node = node_load(arg(1));
  if ($node->type == 'forum') {
    return TRUE;
  }
}
return FALSE;
?>
```

5. A variation: Display a Block throughout all Blogs:

```php
<?php
if (arg(0) == 'blog') {
  return TRUE;
}
if (arg(0) == 'node' && ctype_digit(arg(1))) {
  $node = node_load(arg(1));
  if ($node->type == 'forum') {
    return TRUE;
  }
}
return FALSE;
?>
```

There is a great deal of flexibility here and you should explore creative use of this feature. While you cannot combine the page syntax, above, with the PHP snippets, you can control your Block display to a very high degree with the use of the PHP visibility snippets above.

In addition to the default Blocks, administrators can also use the Blocks manager to define custom Blocks—through use of the Add Block tab at the top of the Blocks Manager.

Theming in Action: Dressing Up Garland

Now, just for the sake of practice, let's take what's been covered in this chapter and apply it to the tailoring an existing theme. We'll start with a default theme and apply the various options available in the system in an effort to create a uniquely tailored theme.

For purposes of the following example, our hypothetical client is Fluid Carbon, a fan site for Italian sports cars. This is a hobbyist's site, so the owner has a very limited budget and doesn't want to pay for custom design work or custom component development; the budget restrictions basically force us to work with Drupal straight out of the box.

Here are the client's requirements…

Look & Feel

- Fluid 3 column layout
- Color scheme to match existing client I.D.
- Must use client's logo in header
- Wants clean look—not too much clutter
- Vertical main nav, in the right column

Functionality

- Blog for site editor (only one blog)
- Forums (only one needed)
- Ability to display third party RSS feed content
- Polls
- Contact form
- Must support user generated comments
- Display button ads
- Site search

The client's requirements are squarely within the capabilities of the default Drupal distro, with only one exception- the need for button ads. Normally, you might want to go ahead and install a banner management extension to handle this task, but this client has no budget, so we're come up with an old-fashioned, low cost (but rather high maintenance!) solution.

Major Tasks to accomplish:

- Modify theme colors to match client I.D.
- Configure theme to match requirements
- Get client logo into theme
- Enable necessary Modules
- Enable new Blocks
- Assign Blocks to create 3 column layout
- Set Block visibility rules
- Create Menu items
- Set user access controls

Along the way, we'll also look at a few little tweaks that will help the usability of the site and add some variety as well. The client is going to load his own content, so for our testing purposes, we'll only create dummy content as needed along the way.

Let's assume for this example, a fresh installation of Drupal. To begin, go to the Theme Manager (**Administer | Site building | Themes**) and click on the **configure** button by the Garland theme. Garland is a fluid design, which supports either 2 or three columns. It is simple and clean and consistent with the client's general wishes. Garland also supports the Color module which makes it easy for us to change the theme color scheme to match the client's existing logo.

Set the Color Scheme

First, let's work on the color scheme. In the configuration manager, select Custom from the **Color set** combo box and enter the values you see in the illustration:

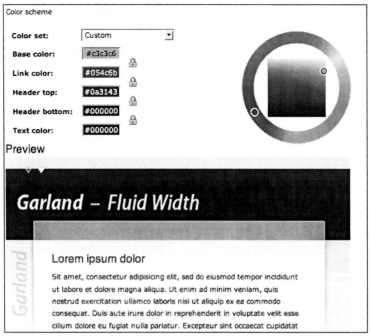

The color module lets you set theme colors from within the admin interface.
As you modify the colors, the Preview image updates

Change Display Settings

Next, scroll down the configuration screen and change the **Toggle display** settings
to enable only the **Logo** option—we don't want the site name, slogan or any of those
other things cluttering up the design.

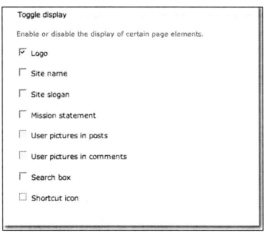

Our Toggle display settings for this example

Upload Logo

The next step is to upload the client's existing logo, by way of the **Logo image setting** controls further down the page in the Theme Configuration Manager.

Logo image settings

If toggled on, the following logo will be displayed.

☐ Use the default logo
Check here if you want the theme to use the logo supplied with it.

Path to custom logo:

files/garland_logo.gif
The path to the file you would like to use as your logo file instead of the default logo.

Upload logo image:

[Browse...]
If you don't have direct file access to the server, use this field to upload your logo.

The client's logo has been uploaded; the system has automatically
named it garland_logo.gif

The client doesn't have a FavIcon and the budget leaves no room to dream one up, so we're through with the Theme configuration manager. Let's save and leave.

Global Configuration

Before we go any further, let's set a few Global options. Go to **Administer | Site Configuration | Site information**. On this page, enter the site name, a slogan (even though you may not intend to set a slogan to appear on the theme, the system still uses it for several purposes, including some page titles!), and the footer, as per the illustration. Note for the footer copy I have not specified the URL for the contact link; if you are using the default Contact module, this URL is always /contact. Once the changes are made, save and exit.

Home › Administer › Site configuration

Site information

Name: *

Fluid Carbon

The name of this web site.

E-mail address:

A valid e-mail address for this website, used by the auto-mailer during registration, new password requests, notifications, etc.

Slogan:

100% fluid

The slogan of this website. Some themes display a slogan when available.

Mission:

Your site's mission statement or focus.

Footer message:

Problems with this site? <a href="#">Contact the webmaster</a>.
Contents released under Creative Commons (CC) License.

This text will be displayed at the bottom of each page. Useful for adding a copyright notice to your pages.

Basic site information is necessary to set the footer and the page titles

Enable Modules

Next let's enable the Modules we need. Go to the Module Manager (**Administer |
Site building | Modules**) and enable the following:

Enabled	Name	Version
☑	Aggregator	5.1
☑	Blog	5.1
☐	Blog API	5.1
☐	Book	5.1
☑	Color	5.1
☑	Comment	5.1
☑	Contact	5.1
☐	Drupal	5.1
☑	Forum	5.1
☑	Help	5.1
☐	Legacy	5.1
☐	Locale	5.1
☑	Menu	5.1
☐	Path	5.1
☐	Ping	5.1
☑	Poll	5.1
☐	Profile	5.1
☑	Search	5.1
☐	Statistics	5.1
☑	Taxonomy	5.1
☐	Throttle	5.1
☐	Tracker	5.1
☐	Upload	5.1

The modules enabled for this example

Manage Blocks

After enabling the Modules, it's time to turn to the Blocks. Go to the Blocks Manager (**Administer | Site building | Blocks**). Then, select the settings for garland by clicking on **garland settings**. The Blocks management for this site takes a bit more time. First, the client requests 3 column and right nav, so I'm going to start by moving the **Navigation** Block from the Left sidebar region to the Right sidebar region.

Next, let's move the **User login** and **Syndicate** Blocks to the Right sidebar, as well. Let's also put the **Search** form on the right and let's activate the **Who's online** Block and put it on the right side as well (that last item is not in the brief but if the client doesn't like it, we can always disable it easily enough!). To cut down on clutter, let's hide the Block titles for the following Blocks: **Navigation, User login, Search** and **Syndicate**.

To hide Block titles, access the Block configuration page for each of the Blocks and enter <none> in the Block title box at the top of the page.

To balance things out on the left side of the screen, let's enable the following and assign them all to the Left sidebar: **Most recent poll, Recent comments, Recent blog posts,** and **Active forum topics**.

 To enable a block, you just need to give it a placement.

To get the placements just right, you can experiment with different settings of the Weight parameter. What I ended up with looks like the illustration.

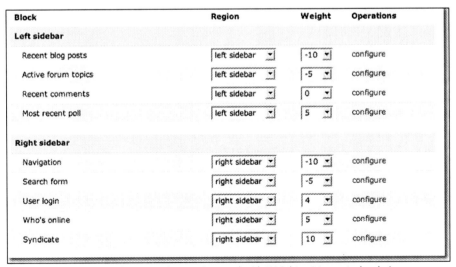

Block	Region	Weight	Operations
Left sidebar			
Recent blog posts	left sidebar	-10	configure
Active forum topics	left sidebar	-5	configure
Recent comments	left sidebar	0	configure
Most recent poll	left sidebar	5	configure
Right sidebar			
Navigation	right sidebar	-10	configure
Search form	right sidebar	-5	configure
User login	right sidebar	4	configure
Who's online	right sidebar	5	configure
Syndicate	right sidebar	10	configure

Blocks enabled, assigned to Regions and with Weight set to control ordering

Add Some Dummy Content and Links

At this stage in the build, it's time to set up some basic containers and materials we need before we can create any menu items. For this client, we need to provide one Contact form and one Forum.

The first step is to create a site wide Contact form. Go to **Administer | Site building | Contact form** and create a contact form with the necessary details.

Next, time to visit the admin side of the Forum and create our client's forum. Go to **Administer | Content management | Forum** and create one forum.

Now it is time to create some navigation links so we can start moving around and loading some dummy content to fine tune the site. From the Menu Manager (**Administer | Site building | Menus**), I am going to work on both the **Primary Links** and the **Navigation**.

On the **Primary Links** menu, I am going to add a new item called "Home" and link it to the front page. I am also going to link into my site contact form on this menu. For the **Navigation** menu, I must enable the link to the forum.

For the next phase, I will load up some sample data to make finalizing the site easier and to facilitate testing. I'm going to create a dummy home page by going to **Create Content | Page**. I'll just use standard Lorem text (generic filler text, typically begins with "Lorem ipsum dolor..." hence the name) and a picture I have of a Ferrari grill to give it some life. Use the **Publishing** options for this item to specify **Promoted to front page**.

Also create a couple of Blog entries, a couple of comments, a phony Poll and a couple of Forum topics—all simply for the sake of checking my Blocks in action and testing as we go.

Set Access Levels

Now that we have some sample content, we need to make sure it is visible to all the right people. This means checking the sites Access control settings. Go to **Administer | User management | Access control.** Configure the settings to enable the following additional functionality for access by anonymous users:

- access news feeds
- edit own blog
- access comments
- post comments
- access site-wide contact form
- create forum topics

- edit own forum topics
- vote on polls
- search content
- use advanced search.

Create a Custom Block

At this stage, the site is coming together and getting close to final form. The open issue on the client's wish list was for button ads. For this one, given the budget, he's getting the low tech solution; I'm going to create a new Block and code the image placement and URL link directly into the Block.

Go to the Blocks Manager and choose **Add Block**. Add a descriptive name and then use simple HTML to specify the image and the URL that it links to. Let's assign this new Block to the Right sidebar, as that column still looks a bit short.

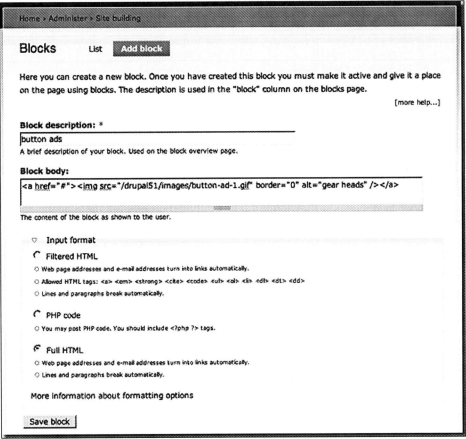

Adding a new (very simple!) custom block to hold the client's button ad image

Note the Input format option is set to **Full HTML** in the example, in order to give more flexibility in use of code in the Block body.

Set Block Visibility

The only thing left at this stage is to configure the Block visibility in a common sense fashion. Let's do the following:

1. Display the User login Block on the home page only
2. Hide the Button ad Block on the administrator pages
3. Display the Recent blog posts Block throughout the Forum posts

First the User login Block. Go to the Blocks Manager and click the **Configure** link on the User Login block. Change the Page specific visibility settings to the second option, **Show on only the listed pages**. In the Pages text box enter <front>; this restricts this Block to displaying only on the front page of the site.

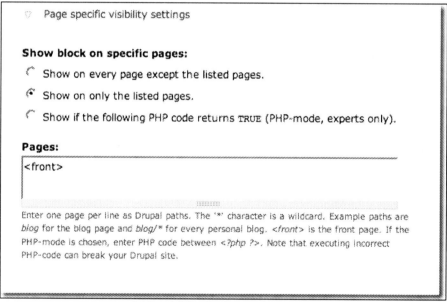

Setting visibility for the User login Block

For the Button ad Block, choose the first option on the Show block specific pages settings, **Show on every page except the listed pages.** Then input into the Pages text box on one line admin and on another line admin/*. The first command bans the Block from the main admin page; the second bans the block from any of the interior admin pages.

Show block on specific pages:

⦿ Show on every page except the listed pages.

○ Show on only the listed pages.

○ Show if the following PHP code returns TRUE (PHP-mode, experts only).

Pages:

admin
admin/*

Enter one page per line as Drupal paths. The '*' character is a wildcard. Example paths are *blog* for the blog page and *blog/** for every personal blog. *<front>* is the front page. If the PHP-mode is chosen, enter PHP code between *<?php ?>*. Note that executing incorrect PHP-code can break your Drupal site.

Settings visibility for Button ad Block

In order to get the Recent blog posts Block to display throughout the Forum posts, but nowhere else, we have to add a bit of logic to help the Block determine exactly which pages are part of the forum. On the Block configuration page, we will need to set the control to the third option, **Show if the following PHP code returns true**, and then add the following code to the **Pages** text box:

```php
<?php
if (arg(0) == 'forum') {
   return TRUE;
}
if (arg(0) == 'node' && ctype_digit(arg(1))) {
  $node = node_load(arg(1));
  if ($node->type == 'forum') {
     return TRUE;
  }
}
return FALSE;
?>
```

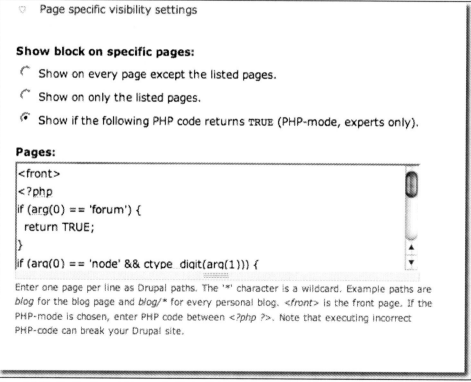

Setting visibility for the Recent blog posts Block. Note that the code in the window is only partially visible here

Taken together, the changes wrought above should produce a site which meets this hypothetical client's initial requirements. Compare the new Fluid Carbon front page with the default garland front page for an appreciation of the difference.

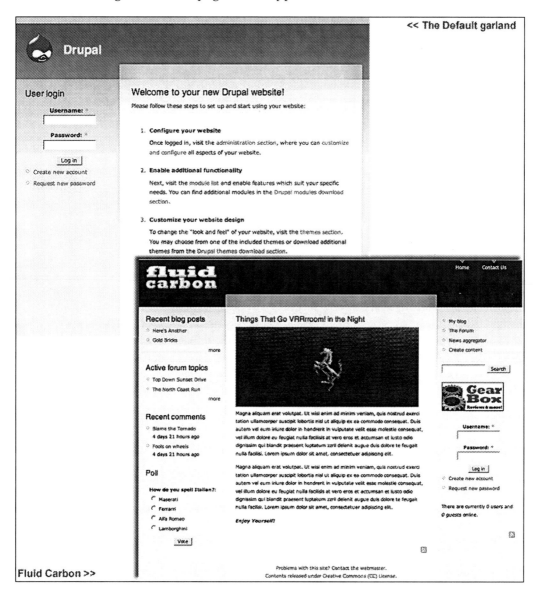

Uninstalling Themes

Uninstalling themes is a simple process, essentially the reverse of installing. First go to the Theme Manager and make sure that the theme you wish to install is not currently enabled. Once you have verified that it is disabled, then access your server. On the server, find the directory containing the theme files and delete the files and the directory. That's all there is to it!

Note that Drupal is very forgiving, and erroneous deletion of an active theme will not crash your site, it will simply result in the content being shown without any styling.

Summary

We started this chapter looking at how to find and install themes and we ended by trying to extract as much as we could from the default system. Given the flexibility of the system it is perhaps not surprising that a number of people work exclusively from the default themes. The Fluid Carbon example in this chapter shows that you can extract quite a bit from the basic set up.

As you will see in the chapters ahead, the techniques we covered in this chapter are just the beginning of what you can do with Drupal themes. Nonetheless, the configuration principles in this chapter, particularly as they relate to the use of Modules and Blocks and the control of visibility settings, are important for all theme work. We will come back to some of these points when we get more into heavy customization and building custom themes, in the chapters that follow.

3
Working with Theme Engines

In this chapter, we will explore theme engines in general and the default PHPTemplate theme engine in detail.

Our exploration of the PHPTemplate engine lays an important foundation for understanding how to create themes or how to extensively modify existing themes. In the examples below, we show the key files used in the process, and how they impact themes. We also discuss the order of precedence among theme files, and how this principle allows us to override the default template files inside individual themes.

We will also discuss the availability of alternatives to the PHPTemplate engine.

Though you don't need to be fluent in PHP to understand this chapter fully, a little familiarity with the programming language will certainly make things easier. The code examples in this chapter come from the Drupal core and the additional themes Gagarin (installed in Chapter 2) and Zen.

What is PHPTemplate?

PHPTemplate is one of a family of applications known as templating engines (referred to frequently in Drupal — and in this text — as "theme engines"). These applications serve a middleware function and determine the coding syntax, which will be used to create the theme. As the name implies, PHPTemplate supports the popular PHP programming language for theme creation.

PHPTemplate was built by developer Adrian Rossouw, and was created specifically for use with Drupal. PHPTemplate is the most widely supported theme engine for Drupal and is compatible with Drupal 4.6 and up. PHPTemplate is included in the default distro of the Drupal 5 series.

Your default PHPTemplate engine files are located on your server in the directory `themes/engines/phptemplate`; additional theme files will appear in the theme directory of each individual PHPTemplate-enabled theme.

 PHPTemplate files follow a naming convention: `xyz.tpl.php`.

For example: `block.tpl.php`, `comment.tpl.php`, `node.tpl.php`, `page.tpl.php`

How does it Work?

PHPTemplate is a tool that helps separate the tasks of the programmer from the tasks of the designer. As a tool, PHPTemplate makes it possible for web programmers to work on the business logic of an installation without having to worry too much about the presentation of the content. In contrast, web designers can focus entirely on the styling of discreet blocks of content and items, comprising the layout and the interface. Developers and designers can divide their tasks and optimize their work.

By comparison, other approaches to theming exhibit less flexibility. Themes can be created only with the use of PHP. Pure PHP themes, however, are difficult for those less fluent in the PHP programming language. Pure PHP templates are also hard to read, more difficult to code, and awkward to preview.

Building themes with a theme engine represents a more manageable way of handling dynamic web applications. Every PHPTemplate theme file contains an HTML skeleton with some simple PHP statements for the dynamic data. The theme files are linked together with the CSS files, allowing the dynamic data to be styled and formatted with ease. In other words, PHPTemplate takes one big step towards the oft-heard holy grail of separating the presentation from the content.

The logic included in a PHPTemplate file is generally rather basic, relying primarily on the use of if statements and includes. Much of the code you will see is even more basic and relates purely to the formatting—CSS styling and basic HTML.

The files contained in the PHPTemplate directory on the server (`themes/engines/phptemplate`) work in conjunction with the files located in the active theme's directory (principally the `page.tpl.php` file) to produce the resulting output. The `page.tpl.php` file is the only PHPTemplate file required to enable a theme to employ the theming engine; likewise, all PHPTemplate themes will have this file inside the theme's directory.

Template files are written in PHP and contain a series of includes and conditional statements designed to detect the presence of elements that must be added into the final output. The includes and conditional statements relate to things like the content of the site title, the presence and location of a logo file, the number of active regions, boxes, etc. Whether a statement is satisfied, and the content displayed, is often the product of decisions made by the site administrator in the process of configuring the site as well as decisions made during the creation of content and functionality.

For example, the segment of code below shows the head of a basic `page.tpl.php` file.

```
<head>
    <title>
        98-*
        <?php print $head_title; ?>
    </title>
    <?php print $head; ?>
    <?php print $styles; ?>
    <?php print $scripts; ?>
</head>
```

The highlighted lines, above, show the include statements in action; in this case, calling into the template file a variety of information including: the page title ($head_title), the head information ($head), the style sheets ($styles), and any necessary scripts ($scripts).

The example below shows a typical application of a conditional statement, again from inside the `page.tpl.php` file:

```
<?php if ($site_slogan): ?>
    <div id="site-slogan">
        <?php print $site_slogan; ?>
    </div>
<?php endif; ?>
```

In this segment, you see a conditional statement testing whether the $site_slogan returns as true (i.e., it exists) and if so, it prints the site slogan ($site_slogan). You will also note that the site slogan is wrapped with a `div` with an `id` of `site-slogan`. This is our first taste of how CSS integrates with the templates to control the presentation on the screen.

Whether the site slogan is displayed is determined by a parameter specified by the administrator in the Theme Configuration Manager (discussed in Chapter 2). The slogan text is set by the administrator in the site information manager. This parameter's value is stored in the database of your Drupal site.

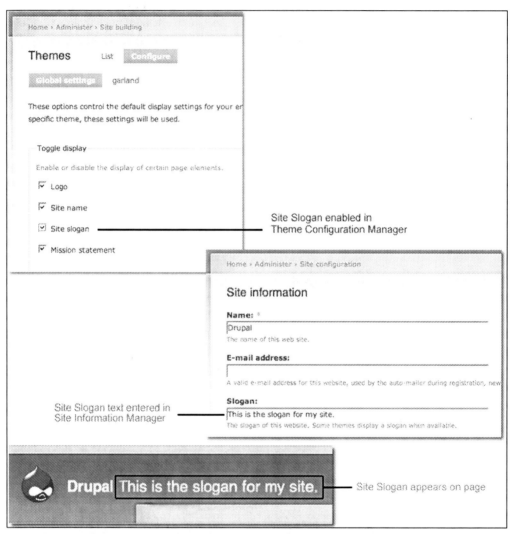

The choices made by the administrator are stored in the database as $site_slogan with the value: This is the slogan for my site. $site_slogan is then displayed courtesy of a conditional statement in the page.tpl.php file.

Putting all this together, it works like this:

1. The `page.tpl.php` looks in the database for the string named `$site_slogan`.

2. If there is a value for `$site_slogan`, `page.tpl.php` then prints that value on the screen.

3. The user's browser applies to the resulting site slogan, the styling specified by the `div` with the `id` `"site-slogan"`.

The `div` styling in this case is located in the file `style.css`, which is also included in the specific theme's directory. Note also that `style.css` is present courtesy of the actions of the PHPTemplate. The style sheets are included via the statement:

```php
<?php print $styles; ?>
```

which appears in the head of the `page.tpl.php` file, as was shown in the previous example.

In summary, a complete Drupal theme consists of a number of template files that are combined at run time to present a coherent single web page. The exact number of templates involved and the nature of their contents will vary from theme to theme.

Getting Started with PHPTemplate

Let's take a look at all the key files involved in a PHPTemplate theme. We will start with the default theme engine files, then look at the key file that unites a specific theme to the PHPTemplate theme engine. To illustrate the principles, we will then look at how two different themes approach their implementation with PHPTemplate.

A Look at the Theme Engine Files

Inside the PHPTemplate directory on the server (`themes/engines/phptemplate`), you will find the following:

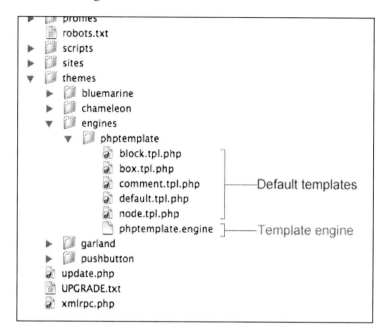

The default template files contained within the PHPTemplate directory provide the most basic level of formatting, necessary for the styling of various page elements. Here's a brief overview of each of the files contained inside the theme engine directory, along with a short summary of their key functionality:

block.tpl.php

```php
<div id="block-<?php print $block->module .'-'. $block->delta; ?>"
class="block block-<?php print $block->module ?>">
<?php if ($block->subject): ?>
  <h2><?php print $block->subject ?></h2>
<?php endif;?>
  <div class="content"><?php print $block->content ?></div>
</div>
```

This template file is used to style the block presentation on the site. Note that the key elements here are the placement of the block subject (note, this is the block's title) and the block's content. The other statements in this file are simply formatting.

box.tpl.php

```
<div class="box">
<?php if ($title): ?>
  <h2><?php print $title ?></h2>
<?php endif; ?>
  <div class="content"><?php print $content ?></div>
</div>
```

This file sets up the wrapping of the content with a "box"—that is, a `div` tag that allows you to format the content along with a title for the box. Note the key elements here are the display of the box's title and the content, each wrapped by styles.

comment.tpl.php

```
<div class="comment<?php print ($comment->new) ? ' comment-new'
: ''; print ($comment->status == COMMENT_NOT_PUBLISHED) ? ' comment-
unpublished' : ''; ?> clear-block">
  <?php print $picture ?>
<?php if ($comment->new) : ?>
  <a id="new"></a>
  <span class="new"><?php print $new ?></span>
<?php endif; ?>
  <h3><?php print $title ?></h3>
  <div class="submitted">
    <?php print $submitted ?>
  </div>
  <div class="content">
    <?php print $content ?>
  </div>
  <?php print $links ?>
</div>
```

This file sets up the display of user-submitted comments to posts and to the forum. Note that the multiple `print` statements here control the display of all aspects of the comment content, including the user's picture, if this option is selected.

default.tpl.php

```
<!-- PHPTemplate was instructed to override the  <?php print $hook ?>
theme function, but no valid template file was found. -->
```

This file is a fallback—a safety net. In situations where a function lacks a valid template, this file is called.

node.tpl.php

```php
<div id="node-<?php print $node->nid; ?>" class="node<?php if
($sticky) { print ' sticky'; } ?><?php if (!$status) { print ' node-
unpublished'; } ?> clear-block">

<?php print $picture ?>

<?php if ($page == 0): ?>
  <h2><a href="<?php print $node_url ?>" title="<?php print $title
?>"><?php print $title ?></a></h2>
<?php endif; ?>

  <div class="meta">
  <?php if ($submitted): ?>
    <span class="submitted"><?php print $submitted ?></span>
  <?php endif; ?>

  <?php if ($terms): ?>
    <span class="terms"><?php print $terms ?></span>
  <?php endif;?>
  </div>

  <div class="content">
    <?php print $content ?>
  </div>
<?php
  if ($links) {
    print $links;
  }
?>
</div>
```

Any time a node is rendered, this file is used. This file is the most complicated of the theme files in this directory, and that is because it does a lot of the heavy lifting on the site; this one file works with all the nodes in their many forms.

block, box, comment, and node (discussed above) are only the basic default functions. There are, however, many additional functions that can be styled using PHPTemplate. A list of themeable functions and their application is included in the Chapter 4.

template.engine

It's an understatement to say that a lot goes on in this file; a review of the source code of this file will go a long way towards helping you gain an understanding of the big picture of how PHPTemplate assembles the output. Unfortunately, a complete dissertation on the inner workings of PHPTemplate is beyond the scope of this book. Accordingly, I have only highlighted two sections that are of particular interest to anyone who wants to understand how to work with themes.

The first highlighted section enables the regions for use in the theme.

```
/**
 * Declare the available regions implemented by this engine.
 *
 * @return
 *   An array of regions. The first array element will be used as the
default region for themes.
 */
function phptemplate_regions() {
  return array(
        'left' => t('left sidebar'),
        'right' => t('right sidebar'),
        'content' => t('content'),
        'header' => t('header'),
        'footer' => t('footer')
  );
}
```

Note that the above section is perhaps the only place where I will ever endorse directly modifying any file contained in the theme engine directory. You may wish to modify this file if you wish to add or re-name a region across multiple themes; in any other circumstance, I strongly recommend that you stay completely away from making changes to these files. If you need to override these files, do so by creating alternative versions of them that are placed inside the theme directory, alongside the page.tpl.php file. This topic is discussed at length in later chapters dealing with intercepts and overrides.

 Note the 't' function in the above excerpt. This function is related to the translation function, which allows Drupal to show the name for the region in the chosen language inside the administration interface.

The second highlighted section is informational. In this excerpt, the order of precedence among template files is defined. The comments in the code here are very useful; note the example showing how the system will respond to a theme file along each element of the path:

```
// Build a list of suggested template files in order of specificity. One
  // suggestion is made for every element of the current path, though
  // numeric elements are not carried to subsequent suggestions. For example,
  // http://www.example.com/node/1/edit would result in the following
  // suggestions:
  //
  // page-node-edit.tpl.php
  // page-node-1.tpl.php
  // page-node.tpl.php
  // page.tpl.php
  $i = 0;
  $suggestion = 'page';
  $suggestions = array($suggestion);
  while ($arg = arg($i++)) {
    $suggestions[] = $suggestion . '-' . $arg;
    if (!is_numeric($arg)) {
      $suggestion .= '-' . $arg;
    }
  }
  if (drupal_is_front_page()) {
    $suggestions[] = 'page-front';
  }

    return _phptemplate_callback('page', $variables, $suggestions);
}
```

The mechanism provided in the example sets out an important principle that is, the order of precedence in the event of the presence of multiple template files. This hierarchy makes it possible for a developer, like you, to create specific templates for specific elements. The option to create themes that can be associated with every element on the path creates a great deal of PHPTemplate's flexibility. Learning to take advantage of that flexibility is one of the key goals of this book.

A Look at the Key PHPTemplate File Contained in the Theme

The template files contained inside the `themes/engines/phptemplate` directory are all linked to another file, `page.tpl.php`, which is located inside the individual theme directory. This file is key to enabling PHPTemplate within a theme.

Some themes use only the basic `page.tpl.php` file to achieve the look and functions the developer desires, others contain a wide variety of additional template files that serve to style specific content or screen space.

For this example, I am using the `page.tpl.php` file from the theme Zen. Zen is not only a representative example of a typical `page.tpl.php` file, but also a particularly useful example due to good use of comments within the code.

```
<!DOCTYPE html PUBLIC "-//W3C//DTD XHTML 1.0 Strict//EN" "http://www.
w3.org/TR/xhtml1/DTD/xhtml1-strict.dtd">
<html xmlns="http://www.w3.org/1999/xhtml" lang="<?php print $language
?>" xml:lang="<?php print $language ?>">

<head>
  <title><?php print $head_title; ?></title>
  <?php print $head; ?>
  <?php print $styles; ?>
  <?php print $scripts; ?>
</head>
<?php /* different ids allow for separate theming of the home page */
?>
<body class="<?php print $body_classes; ?>">
  <div id="page">
    <div id="header">
      <div id="logo-title">

        <?php print $search_box; ?>
        <?php if ($logo): ?>
          <a href="<?php print $base_path;
                          ?>" title="<?php print t('Home'); ?>">
            <img src="<?php print $logo;
                    ?>" alt="<?php print t('Home'); ?>" id="logo" />
          </a>
        <?php endif; ?>

        <div id="name-and-slogan">

        <?php if ($site_name): ?>
          <h1 id='site-name'>
            <a href="<?php print $base_path ?>"
                        title="<?php print t('Home'); ?>">
              <?php print $site_name; ?>
            </a>
```

```
      </h1>
    <?php endif; ?>
    <?php if ($site_slogan): ?>
      <div id='site-slogan'>
        <?php print $site_slogan; ?>
      </div>
    <?php endif; ?>
    </div> <!-- /name-and-slogan -->
  </div> <!-- /logo-title -->

  <div id="navigation" class="menu <?php if ($primary_links)
      { print "withprimary"; } if ($secondary_links)
      { print " withsecondary"; } ?> ">
    <?php if ($primary_links): ?>
      <div id="primary" class="clear-block">
        <?php print theme('menu_links', $primary_links); ?>
      </div>
    <?php endif; ?>
    <?php if ($secondary_links): ?>
      <div id="secondary" class="clear-block">
        <?php print theme('menu_links', $secondary_links); ?>
      </div>
    <?php endif; ?>
  </div> <!-- /navigation -->
  <?php if ($header || $breadcrumb): ?>
    <div id="header-region">
      <?php print $breadcrumb; ?>
      <?php print $header; ?>
    </div>
  <?php endif; ?>


</div> <!-- /header -->
<div id="container" class="clear-block">
  <?php if ($sidebar_left): ?>
    <div id="sidebar-left" class="column sidebar">
      <?php print $sidebar_left; ?>
    </div> <!-- /sidebar-left -->
  <?php endif; ?>
  <div id="main" class="column"><div id="squeeze">
    <?php if ($mission): ?><div id="mission"><?php print $mission;
                                        ?></div><?php endif; ?>
    <?php if ($content_top):?><div id="content-top"><?php print
$content_top; ?></div><?php endif; ?>
```

```
<?php if ($title): ?><h1 class="title"><?php print $title;
                                      ?></h1><?php endif; ?>
<?php if ($tabs): ?><div class="tabs"><?php print $tabs;
                                      ?></div><?php endif; ?>
<?php print $help; ?>
<?php print $messages; ?>
<?php print $content; ?>
<?php print $feed_icons; ?>
<?php if ($content_bottom): ?><div id="content-bottom"><
            ?php print $content_bottom; ?></div><?php endif; ?>
      </div></div> <!-- /squeeze /main -->
      <?php if ($sidebar_right): ?>
        <div id="sidebar-right" class="column sidebar">
          <?php print $sidebar_right; ?>
        </div> <!-- /sidebar-right -->
      <?php endif; ?>
    </div> <!-- /container -->
    <div id="footer-wrapper">
      <div id="footer">
        <?php print $footer_message; ?>
      </div> <!-- /footer -->
    </div> <!-- /footer-wrapper -->
    <?php print $closure; ?>
  </div> <!-- /page -->
</body>
</html>
```

 You can download your own copy of the Zen theme from
http://drupal.org/project/zen.

Let's break down this template file, and look at it in bite-sized functional units (we'll leave the CSS until next chapter):

The following code creates the head of the resulting page. The PHP statements in this excerpt include in the resulting web page: the page title, the various bits of head data including the metadata, the style sheets, and the scripts:

```
<head>
  <title><?php print $head_title; ?></title>
<?php print $head; ?>
<?php print $styles; ?>
<?php print $scripts; ?>
</head>
```

This next excerpt begins just inside the beginning of the body of the page The PHP statements here are all conditional — they will only produce output visible to the viewer when the conditions are true. This section includes the optional items controlled by the site administrator, such as the search box, the logo, the site name, and the site slogan. If the administrator has not enabled any of these items, they will not be displayed on the page:

```
<div id="logo-title">
        <?php print $search_box; ?>
        <?php if ($logo): ?>
          <a href="<?php print $base_path;
                          ?>" title="<?php print t('Home'); ?>">
            <img src="<?php print $logo;
                    ?>" alt="<?php print t('Home'); ?>" id="logo" />
          </a>
        <?php endif; ?>


        <div id="name-and-slogan">

        <?php if ($site_name): ?>
          <h1 id='site-name'>
            <a href="<?php print $base_path ?>"
                              title="<?php print t('Home'); ?>">
              <?php print $site_name; ?>
            </a>
          </h1>
        <?php endif; ?>

        <?php if ($site_slogan): ?>
          <div id='site-slogan'>
            <?php print $site_slogan; ?>
          </div>
        <?php endif; ?>

        </div> <!-- /name-and-slogan -->

    </div> <!-- /logo-title -->
```

This excerpt shows this theme's handling of the navigation:

```
<div id="navigation" class="menu <?php if ($primary_links) { print
"withprimary"; } if ($secondary_links) { print " withsecondary"; } ?>
">
```

The following lines relate to the display of the primary links:

```php
<?php if ($primary_links): ?>
  <div id="primary" class="clear-block">
    <?php print theme('menu_links', $primary_links); ?>
  </div>
<?php endif; ?>
```

The next segment deals with the secondary links:

```php
<?php if ($secondary_links): ?>
  <div id="secondary" class="clear-block">
    <?php print theme('menu_links', $secondary_links); ?>
  </div>
<?php endif; ?>
</div> <!-- /navigation -->
```

This excerpt shows the display of the breadcrumb trail. It also shows the first of this theme's regions, in this case, the header region. In this theme, the header region is declared and active, enabling the site administrator to assign blocks to the region:

```php
<?php if ($header || $breadcrumb): ?>
    <div id="header-region">
      <?php print $breadcrumb; ?>
      <?php print $header; ?>
    </div>
<?php endif; ?>
```

> Note that activating a region has two pre-requisites: it must be placed in the page.tpl.php file, and the region must also be declared in the template.engine file. Adding additional regions to a theme is discussed in detail in later chapters.

This short statement places the left sidebar region on the page. As this theme uses a conditional statement to place this left-hand column on the page, the column will neatly collapse and disappear from view if nothing is assigned to the space:

```php
<?php if ($sidebar_left): ?>
    <div id="sidebar-left" class="column sidebar">
      <?php print $sidebar_left; ?>
    </div> <!-- /sidebar-left -->
<?php endif; ?>
```

This busy excerpt shows a number of events, all of which are associated with the presentation of content items. The statements relate the display of information and functionality with the main content area of the theme:

```
<div id="main" class="column"><div id="squeeze">
```

First is a conditional statement that will display the mission statement (if there is one and it has been enabled by the site administrator):

```
<?php if ($mission): ?><div id="mission"><
                ?php print $mission; ?></div><?php endif; ?>
```

The next line places the `content top` region on the page:

```
<?php if ($content_top):?><div id="content-top"><?php print $content_
top; ?></div><?php endif; ?>
```

Next, comes the Item's title:

```
<?php if ($title): ?><h1 class="title"><?php print $title;
                ?></h1><?php endif; ?>
```

then, the Tabs:

```
<?php if ($tabs): ?><div class="tabs"><?php print $tabs;
                ?></div><?php endif; ?>
```

Next, comes the Help link:

```
<?php print $help; ?>
        <?php print $messages; ?>
```

The next line places the `content` region on the page:

```
<?php print $content; ?>
```

This places the feed icons:

```
<?php print $feed_icons; ?>
```

The next segment inserts the `content bottom` region on the page. This region, and the `content top` region appear often in themes. The `content top` and `content bottom` regions are typically used by the Drupal system in the layout of certain content items; these regions are not generally available for assignment of blocks:

```
<?php if ($content_bottom): ?><div id="content-bottom"><
                ?php print $content_bottom; ?></div><?php endif; ?>
        </div></div> <!-- /squeeze /main -->
```

In later chapters, we will look at how to enable these regions and make them eligible for block assignment.

This excerpt places the right sidebar region on the page. As this theme uses a conditional statement to place this right-hand column on the page, the column will neatly collapse and disappear from view if nothing is assigned to the space:

```
<?php if ($sidebar_right): ?>
      <div id="sidebar-right" class="column sidebar">
        <?php print $sidebar_right; ?>
      </div> <!-- /sidebar-right -->
    <?php endif; ?>
```

This excerpt places the footer region on the page, and also the footer message, if the administrator has included one:

```
<div id="footer-wrapper">
     <div id="footer">
       <?php print $footer_message; ?>
     </div> <!-- /footer -->
   </div> <!-- /footer-wrapper -->
```

Two Contrasting Examples

As you can probably see, PHPTemplate presents a number of options that can be used to support the creation of themes. You can almost literally do as much or as little as you like.

A look at the range of techniques used by the themes in the market shows a wide variety of approaches to theming. Some themes, like the Gagarin theme we installed in Chapter 2, take a very elemental approach and implement only the bare minimum. Other themes, like the default theme Garland, are more complex, and include optional elements.

A Basic PHPTemplate Theme—Gagarin

The Gagarin theme, shown in the following screenshot, in contrast to Garland, shows the most direct and basic approach to the creation of a PHPTemplate theme. If you check the `sites/all/themes/gagarin` directory on the server, you will find the following files:

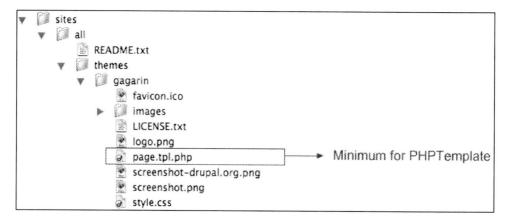

Notice that the creator of Gagarin has chosen to create his theme using the minimum of interaction with the theme engine files. He has used only the `page.tpl.php` file—the bare minimum for enabling PHPTemplate within a theme. He has created no files that intercept or override the default theme files contained in the theme engine directory. Accordingly, the default template files located in the theme engine directory will be used to style the various elements, blocks, boxes, comments, and nodes.

Themes like Gagarin derive their variety from the creative application of CSS.

Themes like Garland derive their variety from both modifying individual theme elements, *and* creative application of CSS.

A More Complex PHPTemplate Theme—Garland

By comparison, Garland shows a more complex approach to the creation of a PHPTemplate theme. If you check the `themes/garland` directory on the server you will find the following files:

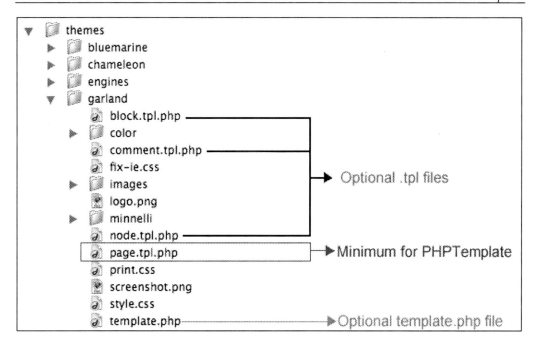

Note here that the theme developer has included not only the required `page.tpl.php` file, but has also included his own versions of some `.tpl.php` files, and another additional file, `template.php`.

The files `block.tpl.php`, `comment.tpl.php`, and `node.tpl.php` that are located in the theme's directory are alternative versions of default files included in the theme engine. The system will give precedence to these files over their counterparts in the `themes/engines/phptemplate` directory. This technique — intercepting and overriding the original files — is what allows theme developers to provide extensive alternative styling and layout. Accordingly, the block, comment, and node elements will be handled by the alternative files in the theme directory, while the box element is still governed by the default theme engine file.

Taking the principle one step further, this theme also includes the file `template.php`. The purpose of this file is to specify additional overrides beyond the basic functions: `block`, `box`, `comment`, `node`, and `page`.

 If you want to override a theme function not included in the basic list (`block`, `box`, `comment`, `node`, and `page`), you need to tell PHPTemplate about it with the `template.php` file.

Alternative Theme Engines

At the time of writing, the release of Drupal 5.x was only briefly past. Developers of the various templating engines were still working to port their applications to Drupal. While the 4.x series sports a number of templating engine options, including the popular Smarty engine and XTemplate, Drupal 5.x users were left with only one alternative to the default theme engine. Engines that are compatible with the 4.x series are not compatible for the 5.x series.

While at this time only one alternative is certified for Drupal 5.x, for purposes of our discussion here, I'll touch on the most popular alternatives to PHPTemplate. Odds are 5.x users won't have to wait for long before the developers of the popular systems below catch up.

PHPTAL

PHPTAL is a PHP implementation of the ZPT system. At the time of writing this text, PHPTAL was the only alternative to PHPTemplate that was compatible with the Drupal 5.x series.

ZPT stands for Zope Page Templates. ZPT is an HTML/XML generation tool created for use in the Zope project (http://www.zope.org). ZPT employs TAL (Tag Attribute Language) to create dynamic templates. Visit the Zope site to learn more about the way of the origins of the system, and how it all works.

TAL is attractive for several reasons. TAL statements come from XML attributes in the TAL namespace that allow you to apply TAL to an XML or plain old HTML document and enable it to function as a template. TAL generates pure, valid XHTML and the resulting template files tend to be clean and easier to read than those created with many other templating engines. One of the biggest advantages, however, is that TAL templates can be manipulated using a standard WYSIWYG HTML/XML editor and previewed in your browser, making the design-work on your theme a relatively easier task.

There are several minor drawbacks to PHPTAL. For purists, it is one level of abstraction further away from PHP, and therefore, performs a bit slower than PHPTemplate (though this difference is unlikely to be noticed by anyone and can be overcome by proper caching). Second, installation of PHPTAL requires Pear5 and PHP5 on your server. If you lack either of these, you should explore other alternatives.

Download PHPTAL for Drupal 5.x at `http://drupal.org/project/phptal`. The Drupal extension includes a variety of extras including at least one PHPTAL theme. You can get the most current PHPTAL snapshot, as well as supporting files, from `http://phptal.motion-twin.com`.

Smarty

The Smarty theme engine allows you to create themes using the Smarty syntax. This popular theme engine is widely used and there are a number of pre-existing themes that are based on Smarty.

Smarty is a mature system and there are a variety of resources to help you learn Smarty's syntax and conventions. Though the system implements another scripting language inside the Drupal system (the Smarty tags), it performs very well. Smarty parses the template files at run time and does not re-compile unless the template files change. Smarty also includes a built-in caching system to help you fine tune performance even further. There are also a variety of plug-ins available, which allow you to extend Smarty's feature set.

Smarty users have been working to get a proper port of Smarty to Drupal 5.x, but at the time of writing, all the efforts were in beta state at best. Nonetheless, given the level of interest and effort, it seems likely a Smarty port for Drupal 5.x will appear soon.

Download Smarty for Drupal 4.7.x at `http://drupal.org/project/smarty`. Smarty's homepage and the most current version of the files can be found at `http://smarty.php.net`.

PHP XTemplate

PHP XTemplate was once the default templating engine in Drupal but has fallen by the wayside as development of the application slowed. For many users, XTemplate was a popular system. It separates the HTML from the PHP and makes it easy for designers to work with themes. Also, as it is written in PHP and can handle either PHP4 or PHP5, it tends to perform well with Drupal.

Unfortunately, at this stage, it seems unlikely to be making a comeback in the near future, and those of you who previously enjoyed using this system should consider alternatives. XTemplate is also released under a different license than Drupal, which may present issues for some users.

Download PHP XTemplate for Drupal 4.7.x at `http://drupal.org/project/xtemplate`. You can visit the project's new home page at `http://www.phpxtemplate.org`. Current files can be found on the SourceForge Project: `http://sourceforge.net/projects/xtpl`.

Installing Additional Theme engines

Additional theme engines can be installed easily. After obtaining the theme engine files, access your server and create a new directory inside of `sites/all/themes`. Name the new directory `engines` and place the theme engine directory inside. Your new theme engine should, in other words, exist inside `sites/all/themes/engines`.

Summary

In this chapter, we've looked in depth at the default PHPTemplate theme engine. You should now have an awareness of the key files involved in a PHPTemplate theme and some appreciation of how those files interact. The discussion of the order of precedence among various theme files lays down a fundamental principle. You have seen example of how to override default theme files by placing alternative files inside the theme directories.

In this chapter, we also spoke about alternative theme engines and noted that although the range of choices is now limited, hopefully we will see more options soon.

Style Sheets and Themeable Functions

All of the HTML output in Drupal comes from various functions, many of which are themeable. The styling of the output is controlled by various style sheets. Accordingly, the key to controlling your site's look and feel is a good command of the themeable functions and the style sheets.

The Drupal system contains a large number of style sheets and an even greater number of themeable functions. In this chapter, we'll take you on a guided tour of all the various style sheets and themeable functions, as a precursor to learning how to intercept and override these elements in the course of customizing your themes.

A Guide to Drupal Style Sheets

A typical Drupal installation will include twenty style sheets, and may also include a certain number of embedded styles. If you have installed additional extensions, you may well find that they come with their own style sheets, pushing the count up even higher.

The Drupal approach to style sheets may initially appear to be overkill in the extreme, or at the very least a rather literal application of modularization, but there is a method behind this madness. The use of multiple style sheets not only makes it easier for the individual module maintainers of the Drupal development team, but also helps you find what you need more quickly than having to deal with one or two massive files. The net result is an approach that is actually quite effective—once you get past the initial shock of discovering twenty-odd style sheets lurking in your system!

In order to reduce the potential threats of conflicting style sheets and absurd loading times, Drupal provides a CSS pre-processing engine. This engine identifies the required style sheets, strips out the line breaks and spaces from all the files, and delivers the styles in a combined single file. The use of this feature is disabled by default; if you wish to use it, you must access **Administer | Site configuration | Performance** and enable the **Bandwidth** option labeled **Aggregate and compress CSS files**.

While working on the themes of your Drupal site, you should make sure the CSS compression is *disabled*. If the compression is enabled, you may not be able to immediately see the impact of changes to your site's CSS.

In the section below, we list the default Drupal style sheets, where they are found, and briefly explain their functions. The contents of each of the style sheets are detailed in Appendix A.

admin.css

/modules/system

Concerns the admin system interface, status reports, and theme configuration.

aggregator.css

/modules/aggregator

Affects the RSS/Newsfeed Aggregator Module and its contents.

block.css

/modules/block

Controls Block formatting.

book.css

/modules/book

Controls the formatting of Book node content.

color.css

/modules/color

Controls the Color module used with some themes. Some styles here affect the Farbtastic function.

comment.css

/modules/comment

Provides the indent style for Comments.

defaults.css

`/modules/system`

Provides styling for basic default HTML elements used throughout the system.

farbtastic.css

`/misc/farbtastic`

Controls formatting of the Farbtastic color picker.

forum.css

`/modules/forum`

Affects the contents of the Forum module.

help.css

`/modules/help`

Styles Help items.

locale.css

`/modules/locale`

Provides a selector for the Locale module.

maintenance.css

`/misc`

Provides styling for the Maintenance page. This is where you can set the "site offline" page.

node.css

`/modules/node`

Provides selectors for Nodes.

poll.css

`/modules/poll`

Styling for Polls.

search.css

`/modules/search`

Styling for the Search module.

style.css

Theme-specific styles — located in the `theme` directory. This is the most critical file in a PHPTemplate theme and is the highest in the order of precedence; styles placed here will override conflicting selectors located in any other default CSS file.

system.css

`/modules/system`

Covers a wide variety of common styles, and also includes menus, tabs, and progress bars.

tracker.css

`/modules/tracker`

Table styles used by the Tracker module.

user.css

`/modules/user`

Styles for the User module and Profile module; includes styles for user administration.

watchdog.css

`/modules/watchdog`

Styling for the Watchdog module.

Identifying Themeable Functions

There is no automated tool for the identification of the various themeable functions in Drupal. You can, however, identify them by their names, because all themeable functions employ a consistent naming convention. Themeable functions' names all begin with `theme_` and they are located in the `modules` and `includes` directories. The naming convention makes it possible to work your way through the various files to isolate all the functions. You can ease the pain somewhat by setting up Dreamweaver or a similar program to do the searching for you.

Additionally, you can use the following snippet of PHP code from within Drupal to produce a list of the active functions on your installation.

```php
<?php
  print '<ol>';
  $functions = get_defined_functions();
  foreach($functions['user'] as $function) {
    if(substr($function,0,6)== 'theme_')
```

```
      print "<li>$function</li>";
    }
    print '</ol>';
  ?>
```

To use this code, first create a new Block within your site. Set the input option for the Block to **PHP**, and then insert the code into the Block body. Give your new utility Block an easy-to-remember name, save it, then assign it to some where you can view the output.

The new Block will print on the screen a list of all the active themeable functions in your system. The snippet is useful but limited; unfortunately, it will not tell you which files to look in to find the functions or exactly what they do.

A Guide to Themeable Functions

With over 125 themeable functions available to you in the default Drupal distro, finding exactly what you need can sometimes be a bit of a challenge. In an effort to simplify the process of isolating relevant functions, we present here a list of the themeable functions, organized relative to the functionality they affect.

Aggregator Module Functions

`modules/aggregator/aggregator.module`

The Aggregator Module provides a variety of functions related to the display of aggregated syndicated content (e.g., RSS, RDF, and Atom).

theme_aggregator_block_item

Formats individual feed items displayed in block.

theme_aggregator_feed

Formats a news feed.

theme_aggregator_page_item

Formats individual feed items displayed on the aggregator page.

theme_aggregator_page_list

Creates an aggregator page listing a number of feed items.

theme_aggregator_summary_item

Formats item heading for summary pages.

Block Module Functions

`modules/block/block.module`

The Block module controls the boxes that are displayed around the main content on a Drupal page.

theme_block_admin_display

Formats the display of the main block administration form.

Book Module Functions

`modules/book/book.module`

The Book module in Drupal allows users to work collaboratively to author a work. The Book module provides the functions that impact Book content and output.

theme_book_admin_table

Finishes up generation of printer-friendly HTML for the Book.

theme_book_export_html

Formats exported HTML.

theme_book_navigation

Formats the links to children and the **previous/next** navigation for a Book page.

Color Module Functions

`modules/color/color.module`

The Color module is related to the Farbastatic module, and provides the color change functionality in the theme configuration manager.

theme_color_scheme_form

Controls formatting of the Color Module form.

Comment Module Functions

`modules/comment/comment.module`

The Comment Module allows users to comment on published content. When enabled, the Comments functionality essentially creates a discussion forum for each node and provides a threaded discussion format within which users can interact.

theme_comment_admin_overview

Controls the formatting of the administration messages for the Update options on comments (i.e., **publish, unpublish** or **delete**).

theme_comment

Handles detailed formatting of comments.

theme_comment_block

Formats the list of recent comments displayed in the Block.

theme_comment_controls

Formats the controls that provide the comment display options.

theme_comment_flat_collapsed

Produces comment in flat collapsed view.

theme_comment_flat_expanded

Produces comment in flat expanded view.

theme_comment_folded

Produces comment in folded view.

theme_comment_post_forbidden

Controls the **you can't post comments** function.

theme_comment_preview

Formats the preview of comments.

theme_comment_thread_collapsed

Produces comment thread in collapsed view.

theme_comment_thread_expanded

Produces comment thread in expanded view.

theme_comment_view

Function for rendering display of a comment. Controls display of first new comment.

theme_comment_wrapper

Allows you to wrap all comments with a `<div>`.

Drupal Module Functions

`modules/drupal/drupal.module`

The Drupal Module uses the XML-RPC network communication protocol to connect your site with a central server that maintains a directory of various Drupal sites. With a Drupal ID, users can notify the central Drupal server about their site, and interact easily with other registered sites.

theme_client_list

Allows for formatting of the list of clients generated by this Module.

Filter Module Functions

`modules/filter/filter.module`

Handles the filtering of content.

theme_filter_admin_order

Themes the filter order configuration form.

theme_filter_admin_overview

Formats the administrator's filter overview form.

theme_filter_tips

Formats a list of filter tips.

theme_filter_tips_more_info

Formats the filter tips **more info** link.

Form Functions

`includes/form.inc`

Handles the various form functions and form elements.

theme_button

Formats a button.

theme_checkbox

Formats an individual checkbox.

theme_checkboxes

Handles a set of checkboxes.

theme_date

Formats the date selection element.

theme_fieldset

Formats a group of form items.

theme_file

Formats a file upload field.

theme_form

Provides an anonymous `<div>` for forms to help satisfy XHTML compliance requirements.

theme_form_element

Returns a themed form element, including the **this field is required** message.

theme_hidden

Formats a hidden form field.

theme_item

Formats a form item.

theme_markup

Formats HTML markup for use in more advanced forms.

theme_password

Formats a password field.

theme_password_confirm

Formats the password confirmation item.

theme_radio

Formats a radio button.

theme_radios

Formats a set of radio buttons.

theme_textarea

Formats a text area within a form.

theme_textfield

Formats a text field within a form.

theme_token

Assists with delivery of a themed HTML string, containing the contents of a hidden form field.

theme_select

Formats a drop-down menu or scrolling selection box.

Forum Module Functions

`modules/forum/forum.module`

Controls the Forum functionality.

theme_forum_display

Formats the forum body.

theme_forum_icon

Formats the icon for each individual topic.

theme_forum_list

Formats the forum listing.

theme_forum_topic_list

Formats the topic listing.

theme_forum_topic_navigation

Provides the **next**/**previous** forum navigation links.

Locale Functions

`includes/locale.inc`

This file works with the Locale Module to enable administrators to manage a site's interface languages.

theme_locale_admin_manage_screen

Themes the locale admin manager form.

Menu Functions

`includes/menu.inc`

Works with the Menu Module to allow administrators to customize the site navigation menu.

theme_menu_item

Formats the HTML output for a single menu item.

theme_menu_item_link

Formats the HTML representing a particular menu item ID.

theme_menu_links

The HTML for primary and secondary links.

theme_menu_local_task

Returns the rendered local tasks. The default implementation renders them as tabs.

theme_menu_tree

Outputs the HTML for a menu tree.

Node Module Functions

`modules/node/node.module`

The Node module allows content to be submitted to the site, in various forms.

theme_node_admin_nodes

Themes the node administration overview.

theme_node_filter_form

Themes the node administration filter form.

theme_node_filters

Themes the node administration filter selector.

theme_node_form

Themes the form used for creating and updating a node.

theme_node_list

Formats a listing of links to nodes.

theme_node_log_message

Styles the log message that appears during node creation and editing.

theme_node_preview

Controls display of node preview for node creation and editing.

theme_node_search_admin

Renders the admin node search form.

Pagination Functions

`includes/pager.inc`

Handles the display of multi-paged content and the related navigation.

theme_pager

Controls display of paged query results.

theme_pager_first

Formats a **first page** link.

theme_pager_last

Formats a **last page** link.

theme_pager_list

Formats a list of nearby pages with additional query results.

theme_pager_link

Formats a link to a specific query result page.

theme_pager_next

Formats a **next page** link.

theme_pager_previous

Formats a **previous page** link.

Poll Module Functions

`modules/poll/poll.module`

Controls the formatting and display of the Polls Module, including the voting forms and the results.

theme_poll_bar

Formats the title and bars in the results view of a poll.

theme_poll_results

Formats the results view.

theme_poll_view_voting

Themes the voting form for a poll.

Profile Module Functions

`modules/profile/profile.module`

Controls the display of user profile information.

theme_profile_block

Prepares the display of a user profile Block.

theme_profile_listing

Themes display of a user profile.

Search Module Functions

`modules/search/search.module`

Enables site-wide keyword searching, and controls display of the various forms and results.

theme_search_block_form

Themes the Block search form.

theme_search_item

Formats a single result of a search query.

theme_search_page

Formats the result page of a search query.

theme_search_theme_form

Themes the theme search form.

System Module Functions

`modules/system/system.module`

Handles all the various configuration controls that help administrators modify the workings of the site.

theme_admin_block

Formats an administrative Block for display.

theme_admin_block_content

Formats the content of an administrative block.

theme_admin_page

Formats an administrative page for viewing.

theme_system_admin_by_module

Themes the output of the Drupal dashboard page.

theme_system_theme_select_form

Displays the theme selection form in the admin section.

theme_system_themes

Formats the listing of themes.

theme_system_modules

Themes callback for the Modules form.

theme_system_modules_uninstall

Themes a table of currently disabled Modules.

Taxonomy Module Functions

`modules/taxonomy/taxonomy.module`

Enables the organization of content into categories, according to a hierarchical vocabulary.

theme_taxonomy_term_select

Displays the default selection field for choosing terms.

Theme Functions

`includes/theme.inc`

This file is key to the Theme system in Drupal and handles a wide variety of theme-related functions.

theme_block

Controls output of a specific Block.

theme_blocks

Controls output of all Blocks in a particular region.

theme_box

Creates a themed box (container).

theme_breadcrumb

Handles the breadcrumb trail.

theme_closure

Formats the `hook_footer()` at the end of the page.

theme_feed_icon

Enables a feed icon.

theme_get_setting

Produces an array containing the settings for a theme.

theme_help

Formats the help message.

theme_image

Themes an image.

theme_install_page

Produces the Drupal installation page.

theme_item_list

Returns a themed list of items.

theme_links

Styles a list of links (such as primary and secondary links).

theme_maintenance_page

Produces the maintenance page ("site offline" page).

theme_mark

Returns a themed marker for content (e.g., **new, updated**).

theme_more_help_link

Produces the **more help** link.

theme_node

Handles nodes.

theme_page

Generates an entire Drupal page displaying the requested content.

theme_placeholder

Formats text for display in a placeholder.

theme_progress_bar

Displays the percentage complete progress bar.

theme_status_messages

Formats status and error messages.

theme_submenu

Returns a themed submenu, typically, displayed under the tabs.

theme_table

Formats a table.

theme_tablesort_indicator

Produces the sort icon.

theme_table_select_header_cell

Controls the header cell of tables that have a select-all functionality.

theme_username

Formats the user name.

theme_xml_icon

Generates an XML icon.

Upload Module Functions

`modules/upload/upload.module`

This module takes care of uploading and attaching files within nodes.

theme_upload_attachments

Displays file attachments in a table.

theme_upload_form_current

Themes the attachments list.

theme_upload_form_new

Themes the attachment form.

User Module Functions

`modules/user/user.module`

Enables the user registration and login system.

theme_user_admin_account

Themes the user administration overview.

theme_user_admin_new_role

Themes the user administration new role form.

theme_user_admin_perm

Themes the user administration permissions form.

theme_user_filter_form

Themes the user administration filter form.

theme_user_filters

Themes the user administration filter selector.

theme_user_list

Produces a list of users.

theme_user_picture

Themes the user's picture display.

theme_user_profile

Generates the listing of a user's account information.

Watchdog Module Functions

`modules/watchdog/watchdog.module`

The Watchdog module provides system monitoring and logging for administrators.

theme_watchdog_form_overview

Formats the display of a page of the watchdog events.

Summary

This chapter contains two valuable resources: a listing of all the style sheets, and a guide to all the themeable functions in the default Drupal distro. The listings indicate where to find the various files and functions and provide you with a brief overview of what the files and functions do.

This marks the end of the introductory materials in this book. These first four chapters have equipped you with all the basic knowledge you need to begin in earnest to modify Drupal themes, and have provided you with the building blocks necessary for creating your own themes.

In Chapter 5, we take the next step and begin to access the style sheets and functions for the purpose of customizing themes to suit our particular needs.

5
Intercepts and Overrides

In this chapter, we dive into the most powerful technique for customizing the output of a Drupal site—the use of intercepts and overrides. The logical consistency of the Drupal architecture lays the foundation for the approaches discussed in this chapter. Through the application of simple naming conventions, you can intercept and override the system's default templates. By creating your own templates and naming them properly, it is a relatively easy matter to gain control over the output of the Drupal site. The techniques discussed in this chapter enable you to change the way pages appear, and dictate different templates for different types of content, or even different users.

Intercepts and overrides can be applied to two different but closely intertwined concepts: Drupal's Cascading Style Sheets (CSS) and themeable functions. This chapter discusses each separately, but the underlying principles that empower the use of intercepts and overrides are exactly the same for both topics.

For the purpose of illustrating the examples in this chapter, we will be using the Garland theme, bundled with your default Drupal distro.

Overriding the Default CSS

The various style sheets within the Drupal distro provide all the style definitions needed to format the site, and the various modules contained in the core. The individual theme you employ may also include additional styles that are particular to that specific theme.

Drupal contains a large number of style sheets—around twenty at the last count! While twenty is certainly a large number of style sheets to juggle, with good planning and use of overrides you can avoid the need to have to track down and modify individual style sheets—remember, we always want to avoid modifying the core files, and that includes the core CSS files.

Drupal is designed to deal with the complexity of this multi-layered approach to CSS gracefully. You can even configure the system to compile the various style sheets at run time, into one coherent list of styles — an option that not only eliminates any potential redundancies but also improves the performance of the site.

The order in which the style sheets are compiled creates a hierarchy. It is not necessary for you to be fluent with the details of the way in which the style sheets are compiled, it is only necessary to appreciate that the order of precedence established by the hierarchy enables you, as a theme designer, to intercept and override the default styles by defining your styles in last style sheet compiled, that is, the theme's `style.css` file.

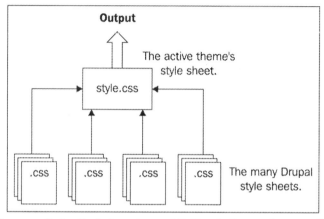

The `style.css` file has the last word—any definitions in the `style.css` file will take precedence over other definitions of the same style. Where there is no conflict, the definitions in the default Drupal style sheets will be applied.

The key factor to keep in mind regarding this hierarchy is that *the CSS inside the active theme directory takes precedence over all other style sheets*. In other words, if there are conflicting styles definitions, the definition included in the theme's style sheet will have control.

 As the name implies, Cascading Style Sheets set style precedence by cascade. The last item in the cascade sets the final output.

If you wish to add additional style sheets, you may do so by creating new style sheets, placing them inside the theme directory, then incorporating them by reference inside your `page.tpl.php` file.

CSS Overrides in Action

Let's take a basic example to illustrate the concept, and show a CSS override in action.

Drupal writes the titles of pages with the class `.title`. The default Garland theme contains no definition for the class `.title`. As a result, the title of page of a default Garland installation appears as in the following screenshot:

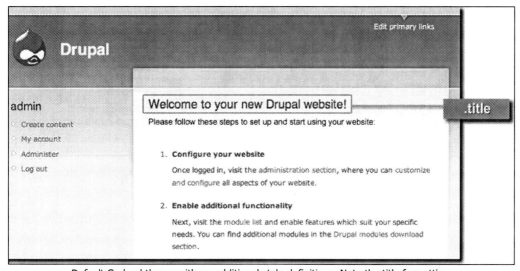

Default Garland theme with no additional style definitions. Note the title formatting.

Let's now add our own definition for the `.title` class into the theme's `style.css` file. Add the following code to the Garland theme's style sheet:

```css
.title {
  color: #666;
  font-size: 1.8em;
  line-height: 2.0em;
  font-style: italic;
}
```

Now save the file to your server, overwriting the original `style.css` file. Reload the page in your browser. The result of the new styling is seen, as shown in the following screenshot:

The result of adding the `.title` class to Garland theme's `style.css` file.

This simple example illustrates the principle — and it really is that simple. There's no need to make changes to the core files and no need to hunt through twenty style sheets to find what you need.

Simply put:

1. Find the styling applied to the item you want to change.
2. Write a new style definition.
3. Place the definition in the `style.css` file.
4. Repeat as needed!

Useful Tool

If you are having trouble figuring out exactly what style(s) you need to change to get the result you want, try using the Firefox browser with the Web Developer extension installed. Among other things, the extension allows you to highlight classes and IDs and even edit live style sheets and view the results in your browser. It is a genuine time-saver. The FireBug extension is also a popular choice, with similar functionality. You can download Firefox at `http://www.mozilla.com`. The Web Developer and Firebug extensions can be found online at `https://addons.mozilla.org`.

Overriding Functions

As discussed in Chapter 3, the themeable functions in Drupal control the HTML formatting for the final display of the contents. You can control the look and feel of the site by modifying the CSS together with the themeable functions. While CSS gives you one level of control over look and feel, to make significant changes to the functionality or the page layout you will need to work with the functions themselves.

The default themeable functions are located in a variety of files inside the distro (see, Chapter 4 for a listing). If your site is using a theme engine, you may also find themeable functions located inside the theme engine directory. Finally, themeable functions may be found inside the active theme's directory.

All themeable functions in a Drupal site can be overridden. As we saw with style sheets, there is a hierarchy at work inside Drupal. The Drupal system will seek out themeable functions in a specific order, and apply the first one it finds.

The themeable function hierarchy is invoked through the use of a naming convention. The default themeable functions can be identified by their names: all employ the nomenclature `theme_functionname()`. For example, the default themeable function that controls the output of a Drupal breadcrumb trail is named `theme_breadcrumb()`.

The default breadcrumb function is located in the `includes/theme.inc` file. We will be looking at this function throughout this chapter, particularly in relation to the way it is overridden in the Garland theme.

Where to Place Overrides

The best practice is to place your overrides inside the individual theme directory. The choice of where you place your overrides is dictated by whether your site employs a theme engine and if so, which one.

PHPTal: Overrides are to be placed in `template.php`.

PHPTemplate: Overrides are to be placed in `template.php`.

Smarty: Overrides are to be placed in `smartytemplate.php`.

 Note that the Xtal templating engine does not permit you to override functions.

At run time, Drupal searches out themeable functions in a specific order. First, the system looks in the theme files, then in those of the theme engine, and finally in the default distro files.

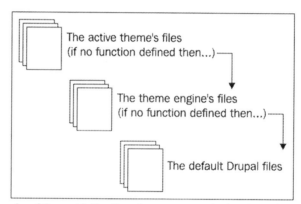

The hierarchy of themeable functions (assumes your site is using a theme engine)

As we saw with CSS earlier, the hierarchy sets an order of precedence that allows you to override functions. However, unlike CSS, where we can override simply by placing a style of the same name in the final CSS file, with themeable functions you must understand and employ the naming convention to achieve the most from this powerful feature of the Drupal system.

How to Name Your Overrides

At run time, Drupal is designed to seek out overrides to themeable functions before applying the default functions. The system does this by looking for files in the following order (assuming your site employs the PHPTemplate engine):

1. `themename_functionname` (e.g., `garland_breadcrumb`)

2. `themeengine_functionname` (e.g., `phptemplate_breadcrumb`)

3. `theme_functionname` (e.g., `theme_breadcrumb`)

The naming convention is the key and must be followed scrupulously, because the name establishes the order of precedence. If the system does not find a function employing either the specific theme or theme engine namespace, the system will apply the default function.

Note that if your site is not using a theme engine, you must use the theme namespace for your override (e.g., `themename_functionname`). If your site uses a theme engine, common practice is to name the function `themeengine_functionname`, but this is not required; either naming convention (`themename_functionname` or `themeengine_functionname`) will work fine.

The advantage of following the `themeengine_functionname` format is portability. By giving the overrides generic names, you can copy them into other themes or even duplicate an entire theme directory as the first step to writing a new theme, all without having to worry about renaming all the overrides.

Overrides in Action: How Garland Works

Let's take as a case study the Garland theme included in the default distro. The author of Garland employs a number of overrides and the way they are implemented provides us with some easily accessible examples of overrides in action. A look inside the `themes` directory shows the structure employed by Garland and gives us hints to this theme's approach to overrides.

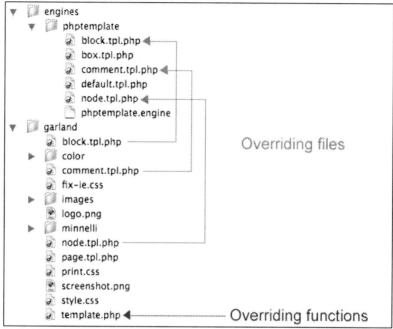

The Garland theme employs a mix of approaches to overriding functions.

Garland employs the PHPTemplate engine that is invoked in the file `page.tpl.php`. Additionally, Garland has provided alternative versions of the following PHPTemplate engine templates:

- `block.tpl.php`
- `comment.tpl.php`
- `node.tpl.php`

The author has also created a new file, `template.php`. The presence of the alternative files and the new `template.php` file indicates that the author has specified variations from the default Drupal presentation. This combination of techniques, providing duplicate templates to supersede the default PHPTemplate engine templates and overriding individual themeable functions, is an example of the two most common approaches to modifying a PHPTemplate theme.

Intercepting PHPTemplate Files

Garland includes alternative versions of several default PHPTemplate template files (`.tpl.php`). The contents of each of those files vary from their counterparts of the same name located in the `engines/phptemplate` directory.

By way of example, let's look at the two versions of the file `block.tpl.php`.

In the original file (located at `engines/phptemplate/block.tpl.php`) you will find the following:

```
<div id="block-<?php print $block->module .'-'. $block->delta; ?>"
class="block block-<?php print $block->module ?>">
<?php if ($block->subject): ?>
  <h2><?php print $block->subject ?></h2>
<?php endif;?>
<div class="content"><?php print $block->content ?></div>
</div>
```

The version of `block.tpl.php` included in Garland looks like this:

```
<div id="block-<?php print $block->module .'-'. $block->delta; ?>"
class="clear-block block block-<?php print $block->module ?>">
<?php if ($block->subject): ?>
  <h2><?php print $block->subject ?></h2>
<?php endif;?>
<div class="content"><?php print $block->content ?></div>
</div>
```

The only difference between the two versions of the file is the class definition in the highlighted line. The Garland theme author has simply substituted a new CSS class to be applied to the blocks. When the Garland theme is active, the Drupal system will apply the Garland `block.tpl.php`, with its new class, and ignore the default file of the same name in the PHPTemplate directory. The modified file in the Garland theme takes precedence over the file of the same name in the PHPTemplate engine's directory.

The author applies a similar approach with the files `comment.tpl.php` and `node.tpl.php`, providing in these files alternative formatting to that included in the default PHPTemplate files. Compare and contrast those files to view the differences.

Overriding Themeable Functions in Garland

In addition to overriding some of the default PHPTemplate engine template files, the Garland author has also chosen to override a number of Drupal's default themeable functions.

To put these overrides into action, the author has created the file `template.php`. This is an optional file, and is commonly used as a convenient technique for grouping together overrides for a number of themeable functions. Whenever the PHPTemplate engine detects the presence of a `template.php` file inside a theme directory, it will read this file first and apply the functions contained therein.

If you open the `template.php` file and examine the contents, you will find overrides for the following functions:

Original function name	Location of original	Garland override's name
theme_breadcrumb	`includes/theme.inc`	`phptemplate_breadcrumb`
theme_comment_wrapper	`modules/comment/` `comment.module`	`phptemplate_comment_` `wrapper`
theme_menu_local_tasks	`includes/menu.inc`	`phptemplate_menu_local_` `tasks`

Let's look in more detail at how a themeable function override is implemented in the Garland theme.

The default definition for the Drupal breadcrumb trail is given in the file `includes/theme.inc`. The default function looks like this:

```
function theme_breadcrumb($breadcrumb) {
  if (!empty($breadcrumb)) {
    return '<div class="breadcrumb">'. implode(' >> ', $breadcrumb)
.'</div>';
  }
}
```

The Garland theme overrides the default breadcrumb function to provide different styling. The override is contained in the file `garland/template.php`. The override looks like this:

```
function phptemplate_breadcrumb($breadcrumb) {
  if (!empty($breadcrumb)) {
    return '<div class="breadcrumb">'. implode(' > ', $breadcrumb)
.'</div>';
  }
}
```

The differences are subtle, but critical. First, the function has been renamed to `phptemplate_breadcrumb` (the developer has adopted the `themeengine_functionname` naming convention in this). The new name alerts Drupal to apply this version of the function, instead of the default `theme_breadcrumb` function. Second, the default function decorates the elements in the breadcrumb trail with a double right arrow (">>"), while the override changes the decorative element to a single right arrow (">"). The result is that the Drupal system recognizes the function placed in the theme file first, and applies a single right arrow to separate the items in the site's breadcrumb trail.

To see this in action, try substituting "*" for ">" in the `phptemplate_breadcrumb` code. Save your modified file and reload the page in your browser. You should see the breadcrumb decoration change from a single right arrow to an asterisk.

Various Approaches to Overrides

The approaches used by the author of Garland are effective, but they are not the only ways of achieving the same result. There are alternative ways to provide overrides. Each of the alternatives has advantages and disadvantages and you, as the theme developer, will need to decide which approach best suits your needs.

The various approaches are:

- Intercepting and substituting files
- Placing overrides in a theme's `template.php` file
- Modifying the PHPTemplate Engine files
- Placing overrides in dedicated template files

In the following sections, we will look at each of these approaches.

Intercepting and Substituting Files

This is one of the approaches we saw implemented by the Garland theme. The essence of this approach is to create a duplicate file for one or more of the default PHPTemplate engine template files. The default versions of those template files are located in the PHPTemplate engine's directory at `themes/engines/phptemplate`. The substitute files must be placed in the individual theme's directory.

 The default PHPTemplate files and their functions are discussed at length in Chapter 3.

Intercepting the default PHPTemplate files allows the theme developer to specify variations from the default presentation of such key areas as blocks, comments, and more.

The Garland author uses this technique to provide alternative formatting for blocks, comments, and nodes.

The process of applying this technique is a straightforward matter of creating a duplicate for the file, and then modifying the code:

1. Create a new file inside your theme directory.
2. Name the new file the same as the PHPTemplate file you wish to override.
3. Copy the code from the original file and paste into the new file.
4. Make your changes to the code in the new file and save the file.

By applying the technique in this manner, you are able to specify your changes without having to modify the original core files. In the future, you benefit from this when it comes to upgrading your Drupal site, because you do not have to worry about the core upgrade overwriting your modifications. Additionally, your modified files are portable: should you wish to apply these changes to another theme, you only need to copy the appropriate files into the theme directory.

Placing Overrides in the Theme's template.php File

The `template.php` file is an optional file in a PHPTemplate theme. When this file is present, the system will look to this file for additional instructions. This file provides a convenient place to define overrides of functions (among other things). Typically, a theme developer will place in this file, all the various function overrides needed for a particular theme.

The use of `template.php` is the most common approach to overriding functions. This approach is implemented by the Garland theme to override the functions relating to the breadcrumb trail, the comments functionality, and the menu.

To apply this approach, follow these steps:

1. Create a new file inside your theme directory (making sure your file includes the starting tag `<?php`).
2. Name the new file `template.php`.
3. Find the functions you wish to customize.
4. Copy the original functions and paste them into the `template.php` file in their entirety.
5. Rename the functions (as per the above discussion).
6. Make your changes to the re-named functions in the `template.php` file and save the file.

Again, this technique allows you to add customization to your site without having to touch the core files, but the primary advantage of this approach is simplicity: one file holding multiple overrides in one location. This approach makes it easy to locate your overrides and manage them. The downside is that this is a theme-specific approach to the issue of overrides; should your site employ more than one theme, this approach may not be optimal.

Modifying the PHPTemplate Engine Files

The brute force approach to theme customization involves changing the template files included in your PHPTemplate engine. The page template files within the PHPTemplate engine directory contain basic formatting applicable to key areas, e.g., blocks, comments, etc. You can modify these files directly, if you so desire.

 This approach involves making changes to the core files of your Drupal site and is not the preferred method of handling customization. I mention this here for completeness, not as a recommendation that you adopt this approach!

The one advantage of this approach is simplicity—no cutting and pasting, no creating new files. Additionally, changes made in this fashion will be available to all themes within the site. In the event you are running multiple themes on your site, this is a quick and dirty way to roll out changes across the entire range of themes. The big downside of course is that you must manage carefully any upgrades to the site, else you risk losing the changes you have made.

Placing Overrides in Dedicated Files

A final technique to consider is the creation of individual template files that are dedicated to overriding specific functions. In this fashion, you employ the function in the `template.php` to call a template file, rather than producing the output itself. This approach is a bit more complicated to set up, but in some cases may be preferable to other approaches.

Drupal functions can be a bit complicated for designers or those less schooled in PHP. This approach allows you to strip down the function to the themeable elements, and do away with some of the confusion that may result from placing functions in the `template.php` file, as discussed above. If, for example, you are a developer working with a designer, you can use this approach to break the themeable elements into bite-sized pieces, and then pass them over to the designer for work on the look and feel. You can focus on the code; the designer can focus on the output.

Creating dedicated files requires additional steps, because you must map the themeable functions to their parallel template files; this is done through use of a PHPTemplate function—`phptemplate_callback`.

The steps are as follows:

1. Create a new `.tpl.php` file inside your theme directory.
2. Name the file logically to reflect the output you will place in this file (e.g., `breadcrumb.tpl.php` would be a logical name for a file holding the breadcrumb trail).
3. Paste into the new file the code from the function that relates to the formatting and the output.
4. Make your changes to the file's code and save the file.

Next, take the steps necessary to map the function to the template file:

1. Create a new file inside your theme directory (making sure your file includes the starting tag `<?php`).
2. Name the new file `template.php`.
3. Find the original function you wish to customize.
4. Copy the original function and paste it into the `template.php` file in its entirety.
5. Rename the function (as per the earlier discussion).
6. Change the function code to call the new template file (created in steps 1 – 4), instead of just the function, and save the file.

This sounds rather complicated, so let's use an example. Suppose the developer of Garland had chosen to create a dedicated file for the breadcrumb function, instead of overriding the output in the `template.php` file. If the Garland developer had taken this approach, it might have looked like this:

1. Create a new file, place it inside the Garland theme directory and name it `breadcrumb.tpl.php`.
2. Enter the following in the new file: `<div class="breadcrumb"><?php print implode(' > ', $breadcrumb); ?></div>` and save the file.
3. Open the `template.php` file.
4. Copy and paste the original breadcrumb function from the `includes/theme.inc` file into the `template.php` file.
5. Rename the function `phptemplate_breadcrumb`.

6. Modify the function to call the new template file, as follows:

```
function phptemplate_breadcrumb($breadcrumb) {
 return _phptemplate_callback('breadcrumb',
 array('breadcrumb' => $breadcrumb));
 }
```

Let's take a look at what happened here and why it works.

As noted at the outset of this section, the essence of this approach is calling a separate template file, in this case `breadcrumb.tpl.php`, instead of placing the function override in the `template.php` file to produce the output directly. Accordingly, the first step is to split out the code relating to the output and put that code into a separate, dedicated template file. The output code is:

```
<div class="breadcrumb"><?php print implode(' > ', $breadcrumb); ?></
div>
```

Note that this is basic HTML styling wrapped around a PHP print statement. The PHP statement in this case controls the display of the breadcrumb (as per the original file), and has been modified to include a single right arrow, instead of the default double right arrow. This sort of basic statement should be relatively easier for many people to deal with, as opposed to trying to extract the output statements from the more complicated function code (as you would have to do if you simply dropped all your function overrides into the `template.php` file).

Now that the output is sorted out and placed in a separate file, the next step is to get the function to call the template containing the output. Since the original breadcrumb function is designed to produce the output directly, you have to modify the code of the function to call the new template. To do this, you have to use `phptemplate_callback`. The `phptemplate_callback` function is how PHPTemplate locates and includes `tpl.php` files. Any time you wish to call a new `tpl.php` file, you will use this function.

In our example, we excised from the breadcrumb function the code that originally generated output and replaced it with this code:

```
 return _phptemplate_callback('breadcrumb',
 array('breadcrumb' => $breadcrumb));
```

 The syntax of `phptemplate_callback` works like this: the first parameter is the name of the function you wish to override; the second parameter is an associative array of the variables you wish to pass with the function.

Intercepting Template Files

Up to this point, we have limited the discussion to how to handle overriding primary template files and individual functions; however, in Drupal, you can extend the intercept and override concept further to achieve highly granular control of the page templates that are called in various situations. You can, in other words, intercept and override entire page files on a conditional basis.

For example, if you wish to have different templates used for different types of content, you can create template files that are displayed when those conditions are met. You can also style individual incidents of modules and other events using the techniques described in this chapter.

The `page.tpl.php` file is one of the most important in a PHPTemplate theme. This file is largely responsible for the results that appear in the browser — it defines the overall layout of the pages of your site. As you might expect given the function of the file, it appears in a wide variety of situations; it is the default page template.

Given the ubiquity of the file, there may well be times when you wish to customize the page that appears to add variety to your site or to enhance usability. Accordingly, the issue then becomes how to intercept the `page.tpl.php` template and override it to display the customized template when certain conditions are met.

Once again, Drupal relies on hierarchies and naming conventions to determine which template is called. By way of example, let's assume you wish to customize the user page. In the absence of any special definitions, Drupal will call `page.tpl.php` when a user clicks on the **My account** link on the main menu of the default distro.

If you want a custom page to be displayed, you will need to intercept the default page and display the page of your choosing. To do so, you will need to create a new template named `page-user.tpl.php` and place it in the active theme's directory. The system will give the file named `page-user.tpl.php` precedence over the default `page.tpl.php`.

Taking this one step further, let's say you want to show a particular user a customized user page. In that case, you would create a new template based on the `page.tpl.php` file and name it `page-user-1.tpl.php` (in this case, displaying the template to the user whose ID=1 when they view the user page).

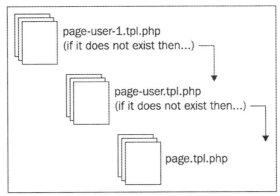

The hierarchy works from specific to general.

Drupal is consistent, and the same logic is applied throughout the system. The system prefers the specific to the general. Drupal looks first for the most specific definition, and where that is absent, cascades downward, finally displaying the default instance where nothing else is found.

The logical, hierarchical nature of the system gives theme developers a great deal of control over pages or elements of pages.

By extension, the same logic can be applied to any `tpl.php` file. For example, a common request is for node-specific styling. To achieve variable styling according to node, you employ the same approach: Create the needed `tpl.php` files (applying the naming convention) and place them in the theme directory. At run time, Drupal will call the appropriate files.

For more information on this subject, as well as examples, please see the discussion of *Dynamic Theming* in Chapter 6.

Summary

Intercepts and overrides are your most powerful techniques for controlling Drupal site output. In this chapter, we covered how to intercept and override both the default Drupal CSS and the themeable functions and templates.

The technique requires an understanding of Drupal naming conventions and an appreciation for the hierarchies that dictate precedence. Proper use of the naming conventions will enable you to extensively customize Drupal's appearance.

This chapter also included a discussion of various alternative techniques for handling themeable functions, together with the advantages of each. Together with good planning, the step-by-step instructions should allow you to implement overrides of themeable functions in a variety of manners.

Modifying an Existing Theme

In this chapter, we will put together the various techniques that we have covered and demonstrate how to modify and heavily customize an existing theme. The majority of people who get into Drupal themes tend to do so by modifying other themes and learning from them; and that's exactly what we're going to do in this chapter.

We will take an existing theme, look at how it works, then copy it and modify it until we have a very different looking theme. In this case, we will be building a fixed width, CSS-based, personal blog theme.

For the purpose of illustrating the examples in this chapter, we start with the Zen theme, which you can download from the Drupal site.

Setting Up the Workspace

There are several software tools that can make your work of modifying themes more efficient. Though no specific tools are required to work with Drupal themes, there are a couple of applications that you might want to consider adding to your tool kit.

I work with Firefox as my primary browser, principally due to the fact that I can add into Firefox various extensions that make my life easier. As mentioned in the previous chapter, installing the Web Developer extension is hugely helpful when dealing with CSS and related issues. I highly recommend the combination of Firefox and the Web Developer extension to anyone working with Drupal themes.

Of course, it must be said that in addition to working with Firefox, you should check your work in all the most popular browsers and across the various devices that your target audiences might employ. Checking your work in only one browser is never sufficient.

Next, when it comes to working with PHP files and the various template files of a theme, you will need an editor. The most popular editor is probably Dreamweaver, from Adobe, although any editor that has syntax highlighting would work well too. Dreamweaver provides a number of features that make working with code easier (particularly for designers). To get the most out of Dreamweaver, you will need to open the preferences dialogue and make some modifications to the configuration.

Specifically, Dreamweaver users will need to configure the application to allow you to edit the various types of files common to PHPTemplate themes. Start Dreamweaver, then:

1. Go to the **Preferences** dialogue.
2. Open **file types/editors**.
3. Add to the field **open in code view** the following:
   - `.info`
   - `.module`
   - `.install`
   - `.pl`
   - `.sh`
   - `.theme`
4. Save the changes and exit.

With these changes, your Dreamweaver application should be able to open and edit the PHPTemplate theme files.

Previewing Your Work

Note that previewing themes is easiest through use of a server. Themes can be hard to preview and it is often easier just to set up a local development server and install Drupal to preview your work as you go. The WAMPP package for Windows (called "XAMPP" for Linux and "MAMP" for Mac), provides a one step installer containing everything you need (Apache, MySQL, PHP, phpMyAdmin, and more) to set up a server environment on your PC. Visit `http://www.ApacheFriends.org` to download WAMPP, XAMPP, or MAMP, and then install it on your local machine and you have an instant Dev Server!

Planning the Modifications

The Zen theme has some of the attributes we're looking for in our final design and is pure CSS. The theme also has a useful structure for tutorial purposes and is well commented. Accordingly, we're going to start with Zen and modify it until we reach our final goal, that is, a new theme we will name "Tao".

You can download a copy of the Zen theme at `http://drupal.org/project/zen`. Note, however, that the Zen theme is under active development and as a result, the version you download today may not be the same as the one used in the examples in this text.

Any time you set off down the path of modifying an existing theme to fit your needs, you need to spend some time planning before you start modifying code. The idea here is simple: a little time spent up front pays off big-time in savings later on.

A dissertation on site planning and usability is beyond the scope of this book, so for our purposes let us focus on defining goals and on satisfying a specific wish list for the final functionality.

In order to make it easy to follow, without having to install a variety of third-party extensions, the changes we will make in this chapter will be done from within the theme itself. Arguably, were you building this for deployment, rather than simply for skill development, you might wish to consider implementing one or more specialized third-party extensions (like a banner manager) instead of re-inventing the wheel as we do in this exercise.

For the example in this chapter, the goal is to create a two-column blog-type layout with solid usability and good branding. The secondary concern is to include space for advertising and a top banner. The theme must also support a forum and a user comments functionality.

Specific changes we wish to implement include:

- Secondary Nav mirrored on top and bottom
- Main Nav in the right column
- Adding top banner space below Top Nav but above branding
- Changing logos, color scheme, and fonts to match brand identity
- Enable blog
- Enable forum
- Enable comments

Cloning a Theme

Let's get started by making a copy of the Zen theme. We'll keep the original and work on the copy. I recommend you always employ this approach to cloning themes: by preserving the integrity of the original, you have a reference and you maintain the ability to roll back your changes in the event a serious problem arises.

Cloning a theme is a simple matter. First, make a copy of the original theme and place the copied directories in the `sites/all/themes` directory. Next, rename the directory with your chosen theme name. In the case of the Zen theme, we also have to re-name the sub-theme, Zen-Fixed, which has its own directory.

Let's name the new primary theme Tao and the secondary theme Tao-fixed. The result of copying and renaming the directory should look like the illustration.

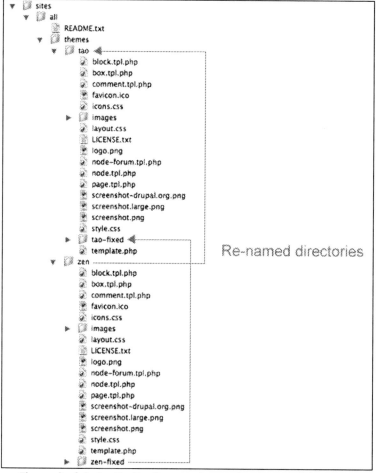

The result of cloning the Zen theme and re-naming the copied directories

After re-naming the theme, it is necessary to re-name any theme-specific functions.

Open the `template.php` file in our Tao directory. As is typical in a PHPTemplate theme, the author has placed the themeable function overrides in the `template.php` file. Search out the functions that use the following nomenclature:

```
function zen_functionname()
```

Substitute our new theme name "tao" for "zen." Hence, `function zen_regions()` becomes `function tao_regions()` and `function zen_breadcrumb()` becomes `function tao_breadcrumb()`. Apply this change to all functions in the `template.php` file and save the file to complete the cloning of the theme.

> Note that if you wish to use the `zen_id_safe` function, after you re-name it you will also need to change the name of references to it in `template.php`.

First Look at Zen/Tao

The files we've copied from Zen are instructive as they provide us with a several CSS files and a variety of approaches to overriding the default themeable functions. There are two variations on one theme here—a variable width version named "Zen" and a fixed width version named "Zen-fixed". Both use the same underlying PHPTemplate files but each has its own `style.css` file to control the layout. We will maintain this structure in our new theme, creating both "Tao" and "Tao-fixed.".

CSS in Zen/Tao

The CSS implementation in the Zen/Tao theme is different from what we've seen in previous themes in two aspects: First, there is the presence of the sub-theme, and second, the theme employs multiple CSS files.

The creation of a sub-theme—a theme within a theme, if you will—is made possible by the way Drupal works with themes. The system allows you to create multiple themes based on the same set of underlying files through the use of an additional CSS file placed within a subdirectory. The same approach used here in Zen (and Tao), is employed in the default Garland theme, which includes the sub-theme Minelli, and in the default theme Chameleon, which includes the sub-theme Marvin.

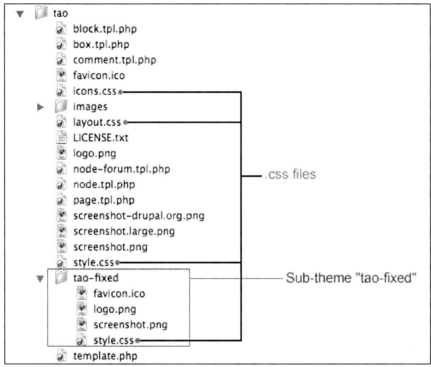

The CSS files of our new themes Tao and Tao-Fixed

Note that, at the most basic, a theme needs only one CSS file—the `style.css` file. In Zen/Tao, we see two incidences of `style.css`: one for the primary theme and one for the sub-theme. Additionally, the author has included the files `icons.css` and `layout.css`; these files are optional and have been created by the theme's author for specific purposes.

CSS file	Function
tao/style.css	Main styling for Tao theme
tao/icons.css	The styling for various icons used in the theme
tao/layout.css	Controls the general page layout and the columns
tao-fixed/style.css	Main styling for Tao-Fixed theme

The theme's author tells the system which CSS files to include by importing the files at the top of the theme's `style.css` file.

 The process of using an import statement to add the styles from one CSS file to another is called "creating a cascade" — hence the name Cascading Style Sheets.

Look at this excerpt from the `style.css` file of the primary theme, Tao:

```
/***    IMPORT EXTERNAL STYLE SHEETS
 *   We have separated out these styles because they are
 *   common to the template system.
 */
@import "layout.css";
@import "icons.css";
```

The last two lines instruct the system to include the additional CSS files.

Now compare the code below, which is from the `style.css` file of the sub-theme, Tao-fixed:

```
/* We need to grab the CSS files from the directory above
 */
@import "../layout.css";
@import "../icons.css";
@import "../style.css";
```

In the code above, the import commands include both the two optional CSS files and the primary theme's `style.css`. Put another way, the primary theme employs a cascade of three CSS files, while the sub-theme uses a cascade of four CSS files, including the primary theme's `style.css` file.

The theme author's decision to split out certain types of styles into the files `layout.css` and `icons.css` is done for convenience and ease of maintenance. The optional CSS files are used to contain style and layout definitions that are common to both the primary and the sub-theme.

`Layout.css`, for example, contains style definitions that are used to control the formatting of the page into one, two, or three columns, and are applicable to both theme variations.

`Icons.css` controls the formatting of various icons used by the system.

To achieve the final design of our new Tao-fixed theme, it will be necessary to make a number of changes to the `style.css` file located in the Tao-fixed directory. But before we begin with that, let's look at the way the themeable functions are handled in the original files.

Themeable Functions in Zen/Tao

The theme includes a `template.php` file which, as we have seen in previous examples, contains various overrides to themeable functions. The author of the theme has also gone further and written files to intercept and override the key template files, `block.tpl.php`, `box.tpl.php`, `comment.tpl.php`, and `node.tpl.php`. Each of those files will override its respective counterpart in the PHPTemplate engines directory. The author has also added the file `node-forum.tpl.php`, which is designed to provide overrides specific to the forum functionality.

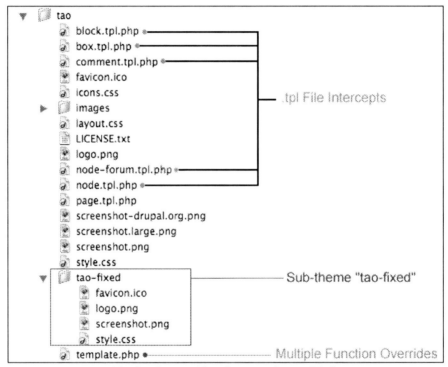

The function overrides of our new theme—"Tao"

Note that all the overrides are shared, and are placed in the root of the theme rather than in the sub-theme directory.

- `block.tpl.php`: This template styles the block presentation.
- `box.tpl.php`: This template provides a container for wrapping the contents.
- `comment.tpl.php`: This template formats comments to posts and to the forum.
- `node.tpl.php`: This template formats the nodes.
- `node-forum.tpl.php`: This template formats the forum.

The `template.php` file contains only one override—the breadcrumb function, which controls the formatting of the breadcrumb trail. The various alternative `.tpl` files provide a narrow range of customizations, largely focusing on inserting additional divs and classes that the theme's author uses to give more control over the formatting of various items.

> Drupal follows rules of precedence in regards to template files, just as it does in other areas (e.g., themeable functions, CSS, etc.). For example, the following list of files goes from most specific to least specific—the files in the upper part of the this list have precedence over the ones below them in the list:
>
> `page-node-edit.tpl.php`
>
> `page-node-1.tpl.php`
>
> `page-node.tpl.php`
>
> `page.tpl.php`

Turning Zen into Tao

The process of transforming one theme into another consists of a set of tasks that can roughly be divided into three parts:

1. Configuring the Theme
2. Adapting the CSS
3. Adapting the Themeable Functions

Configuring the Theme

To begin the process of changing the Zen theme into our new Tao design, the first step is to enable the needed modules, blocks, and other configuration settings. As stated previously, the goal of this re-design is to create a blog theme with solid usability and a clean look and feel. The resulting site will need to support forums and comments and will need advertising space.

Let's start by enabling the functionality we need and then dropping in some sample contents so we can see the effects of what we are doing with the CSS and the themeable functions.

The first step is to enable our new theme. Go to the Themes Manager, and enable the theme **Tao-fixed**. Set it to be the default and save the changes.

Now we're set to begin customizing this theme.

Set Global and Theme Configuration Options

Let's start by logging in as an administrator and then applying the relevant global configuration settings we need.

First, navigate to the **Site Information** screen (**Administer | Site configuration | Site information**). Rename the site from **Drupal** to **Tao-Fixed** and then let's add a slogan: **A fixed width CSS blog theme based on Zen.** Save your changes and let's move on to the next step.

Go to the Theme-specific configuration settings for Tao-Fixed. Enable the **Site slogan** and the **Search box**. While we're here, also disable the mission statement, the logo, and the shortcut icon options. Save your changes.

 More detailed information on the configuration options applicable to Themes can be found in Chapter 2.

Enable Modules

Our new Tao theme contemplates the use of several functionalities that are not enabled by default. Accordingly, before we can go too far, we need to enable the modules we wish to use.

Access the Module Manager, and on that screen enable the following Modules:

- Search
- Forum
- Contact
- Blog
- Comment

 More detailed information on the use of Modules can be found in Chapter 2.

Save your changes.

Set User Access

We now need to set the user permissions so that our site visitors can see and use the various functionalities we've set up.

Go to the **User management** section and open the **Access control** manager. Select the following for anonymous user access:

- Access comments
- Post comments
- Access site-wide contact form
- Access content
- Search content

Save your new permissions and let's move on to the next step in our preliminary preparations.

Create Dummy Content

Temporary dummy content allows us to see text on the screen as we make our changes, and helps us to judge more easily our fonts, colors, spacing, and margins.

First, let's create a new Page. Name it **About Us** and throw in a few lines of placeholder text. Next, create a couple of Blog entries with dummy text. Finally, let's add a new Forum. To do this, access the **Forums** option under **Content Management**. You will see there a message advising you that you need to create a new forum in order to activate fully this module. Let's add a new forum and name it simply **New**. This is sufficient for our needs at this stage.

Now that we have our modules, some sample content, and a forum in place, it's time to set up some menu choices to connect these items to the navigation.

Set Up Menus

For this theme, we're going to run the Primary Links at the top of the page. We'll set the menu named Navigation as our Main Nav on the right-hand side of the page. We'll also create a Footer Nav and place that at the bottom of the page.

Access the Menu manager, under **Site building**, and make the changes outlined below.

For the Primary Links, we will need to set up the following (note that the Weight settings, which affect the ordering, are completely up to you; these are simply suggestions):

Name for Link	Path (URL)	Weight
Home	`<front>`	10
Contact Us	`yourdomain/?q=contact`	-10

For the Navigation Menu, set up the following:

Name for Link	Path (URL)	Weight
Blog Entries	`yourdomain/?q=blog`	10
About Us	`yourdomain/?q=node/` `(node number)`	0
Forums	`yourdomain/?q=forum`	10

For the navigation on the footer, we'll have to do a bit more, because this menu does not exist and will need to be created before we can go about adding links. The first step is to select the **Add menu** tab on the Menu manager; entitle your new menu **Footer** and click **Submit**. Next, let's set up the links we want on the Footer nav:

Name for Link	Path (URL)	Weight
Home	<front>	10
Login	`yourdomain /?q=user`	0
Contact Us	`yourdomain /?q=contact`	-10

Two more steps remain to complete this task. First, let's disable the default Primary and Secondary Menu displays and manage this manually. To do this, go to the Menu manager and select the **Settings** tab. On the Setting screen set the combo box labeled **Menu containing primary links** to **No primary links**. Set the combo box labeled **Menu containing secondary links** to **No secondary links**. Save your changes.

Finally, since we added a link to the Login box to our Footer Nav, let's hide the display of the Login Block to keep our screen clear of clutter. To do this, visit the Block manager and select the Region for the **User login** Block to **<none>**. Save your changes and we have finished this task.

Add New Regions

The Tao theme requires the addition of a horizontal navigation menu that hangs from the top of the page and the ability to insert banner ads. As these areas of the page are planned to be distinct in their usage and in their formatting, it is probably best to create new Regions for these purposes.

To provide space for our requirements, we will be adding two new regions, named **page_top** and **banner**. Before we go any further with the configuration, we need to create these Regions so that they are available for Block placement.

Adding new Regions to a theme is a two-step process: You must modify the Regions function to include the new Regions and then you must place the code that includes the Regions into the page.tpl file.

As discussed in Chapter 3, the PHPTemplate engine by default makes the following regions available to all themes:

- left
- right
- content
- header
- footer

These regions are set in the phptemplate.engine file.

```
function phptemplate_regions() {
  return array(
  'left' => t('left sidebar'),
  'right' => t('right sidebar'),
  'content' => t('content'),
  'header' => t('header'),
  'footer' => t('footer')
  );
}
```

The function in the phptemplate.engine file can either be modified directly (not recommended!) or overridden at the individual theme level. In this case, we only want to add the regions for this one particular theme, therefore, we will simply override the function in the template.php file.

To add our new Regions, open the file `tao/template.php` with Dreamweaver, or your editor of choice, and find the following code:

```
function tao_regions() {
  return array(
  'left' => t('left sidebar'),
  'right' => t('right sidebar'),
  'content_top' => t('content top'),
  'content_bottom' => t('content bottom'),
  'header' => t('header'),
  'footer' => t('footer')
  );
}
```

The `tao_regions` function in the `template.php` file will supersede the `phptemplate_regions` function in the `phptemplate.engine` file. The theme author has already defined two new regions for use in this theme: `content_top` and `content_bottom`. (Note as well that the default region **content** is not defined here — it has been removed.)

Now, let's add to that function our two new regions, **page_top** and **banner**, as follows:

```
function tao_regions() {
  return array(
  'page_top' => t('page top'),
  'banner' => t('banner'),
   'left' => t('left sidebar'),
  'right' => t('right sidebar'),
  'content_top' => t('content top'),
  'content_bottom' => t('content bottom'),
  'header' => t('header'),
  'footer' => t('footer')
  );
}
```

Save your `template.php` file to conclude the first part of this task.

The second step is to place the Regions' code into the `page.tpl.php` file, so the Regions can be positioned and styled. For Tao-Fixed, the plan is to use the Region Page Top to hold a Top Nav that hangs from the top of each page. The Banner Region is to be placed below the Page Top and before the existing Header Region.

Open Tao's `page.tpl.php` file. Note the following code, immediately after the head of the document:

```
<body class="<?php print $body_classes; ?>">
  <div id="page">
   <div id="header">
      <div id="logo-title">
```

We're going to modify that to include our two new Regions, as follows:

```
<body class="<?php print $body_classes; ?>">
  <div id="page">
   <div id="page-top">
     <?php print $page_top; ?>
   </div>
   <div id="banner">
     <?php print $banner; ?>
   </div>
      <div id="header">
          <div id="logo-title">
```

Note that I have wrapped both the statements that include the new Regions with divs. To make them easy to remember, name the `id` of each `div` to match the Region. When we modify the CSS later, we will define these new divs to set the position and formatting of the contents of these Regions.

Enable and Configure Blocks

Let's enable three of our default Blocks: **Recent comments**, **Syndicate**, and **Who's online**. We will add some more items and configure them later, but for now we need only these three. Let's assign all three to the region **Right Sidebar**. Put them in whatever order you like. I set them up in this example with Navigation at the top, followed in order by **Recent comments**, **Who's online**, and **Syndicate**.

While you're here, hide some of the Block titles that we don't want to see on the page. Open the configure dialogue for the **Syndicate** block and set the **Block title** to **<none>**. Do the same with the **Primary Links**, **Footer**, and **Navigation** Blocks.

One of the requirements for this theme was the provision of space for a banner ad at the top of the pages. For our purposes, we're going to set up the banner the crude way—that is, we're going to create a Block for the banner, then hard-code the location of the banner image into the Block.

To provide a dummy banner image that we can work with, I downloaded a sample leaderboard and then placed it in the `images` directory inside our theme. I will link to the sample banner image for testing purposes. Later, the user can either employ this banner block or they can find an alternative approach for placing a banner in this position. Either way, the styling will be in place and the site ready to accommodate the ads.

> The Internet Advertising Bureau maintains an online collection of sample ads units in various official sizes; this is a good resource for placeholders. For our Tao-Fixed theme, I have downloaded a sample Full Leaderboard ad unit: 728 x 90 pixels, `http://www.iab.net/standards/adunits.asp`.

To create our new Block, access the Block Manager and choose **Add Block**. Name your new Block **banner**. Next, insert a link to the banner image in the **Block Body** text field, as follows:

```
<a href="#" ><img src="(yoursiteURL)/sites/all/themes/tao/images/
728x90.gif" /></a>
```

Set your input format to Full HTML, and then finally chose **Save block**. Assign this Block to the Region **Banner**. Finally, click the configure link next to this Block and set the **Block Title** field to **<none>** to complete this operation.

> If this were a production site, rather than a basic demo, I would approach the actual banner management in a different fashion: If I were using Google AdSense on the site, I would use the Block Body to input my AdSense code. If, on the other hand, I needed more complete banner management functionality, such as the ability to run my own ads, control display, and generate reports, I would install a third-party extension and follow its instructions for implementing the Block. A number of extensions provide extended ad management functionality, see `http://drupal.org/project/Modules/category/55` for a list.

Position Blocks

Let's go ahead now and assign the Blocks to the Regions in which we want them to appear.

Access the Blocks Manager screen. Note that if you added your Regions successfully, you will see the new Regions highlighted in yellow on this screen. Additionally, if you check the Region drop down, you should now see our two new Regions are listed as **Page Top** and **Banner**.

Assign the **Primary Links** to **Page Top**, the **Navigation** to **Right Sidebar**, and the **Footer** to the Region **Footer**. Your navigation is now in place; now, let's position the remaining Blocks as follows:

Name for Block	Region
Banner	Banner
Footer Nav	Footer
Primary Links	Page top
Navigation	Right sidebar
Recent Comments	Right sidebar
Who's Online	Right sidebar
Syndicate	Right sidebar

At this point in the process, we have all the basics in place. The system is set up with the basic configuration and the new Regions in place. The various Modules are enabled, the Menus populated, and the output Blocks positioned as we want them to be in the final site. At this time, the site is visually a bit of a mess, but now that all the elements are visible we can start on the CSS and the particular customizations required to achieve our final design.

 More detailed information on the use of Blocks can be found in Chapter 3.

Adapting the CSS

As we saw earlier in this chapter, the Tao-Fixed theme relies upon a cascade of four separate style sheets. Unfortunately, the various styles we need to modify do not appear in one place; they are scattered among the four style sheets. The good news is that we need not concern ourselves with hacking away at all four style sheets, we can instead place all our changes in the Tao-Fixed `style.css`, because the system will give precedence to the styles defined in this file, in the event of any conflicting definitions.

Precedence and Inheritance

Where one style definition is in an imported style sheet and another in the immediate style sheet, the rule in the immediate style sheet (the one that is importing the other style sheet) takes precedence.

Where repetitive definitions are in the same style sheet, the one furthest from the top of the style sheet takes precedence in the case of conflicts.

Where repetitive definitions are in the same style sheet, non-conflicting attributes will be inherited.

Open up the `tao-fixed/style.css` file and alter it as follows.

Setting the Page Dimensions

For this exercise, I wanted to make a fixed width theme optimized for display settings of 1024 x 768. The Zen-Fixed theme is optimized for the smaller 800 x 600 screen. Accordingly, one of the most basic changes we need to make is to the page dimensions. The entire page area is wrapped with a `div` with the `id=page`.

Let's modify the selector `#page`. The `tao/style.css` file contains the following `#page` settings—commented out:

```
#page {
    /*width: 900px;   */              /* page width - optional */
    /*margin: 0 auto;   */            /* center the page - optional */
    /*border-left: 2px solid #AAA;*/
    /*border-right: 2px solid #AAA;*/
}
```

In the Zen theme, the author was kind enough to provide alternatives for the page formatting. All we need to do to take advantage of this convenient bit of work is to remove the comment marks and adjust as we desire. Let's copy that, paste it into our `tao-fixed/style.css` and modify it as follows:

```
#page {
    width: 980px;
    margin: 0 auto;
    border-left: 4px solid #666633;
    border-right: 4px solid #666633;
}
```

In this case, I set page width to 980 pixels, a convenient size that works consistently across systems, and applied the margin attribute to center the page. I have also applied the `border-left` and `border-right` styles and set their color and width.

Formatting the New Regions

Let's begin by positioning and formatting the two new Regions, Page Top and Banner.

When we placed the two new Regions in our `page.tpl.php` file, we wrapped them both with divs. Page Top was wrapped with the div `page-top`, so let's create that in our `style.css` file:

```
#page-top {
margin: 0;
background-color: #676734;
```

```
width: 980px;
height: 25px;
text-align: right;
}
```

The Region banner was wrapped with the div `banner`, so let's now define that selector as well:

```
#banner {
background-color: #fff;
width 980px;
height: 90px;
text-align: center;
}
```

Fonts and Colors

Some of the simplest CSS work is also some of the most important — setting font styles and the colors of the elements.

Let's start by setting the default fonts for the site. I'm going to use this as a chance to consolidate the `body` tag definition into the theme's `style.css`, and also modify the `div` with the id `page`.

There are several body tags contained in the `tao/style.css`. I am going to cut them and paste them and combine them into one `body` tag in our `tao-fixed/style.css` file. We wind up with this:

```
body {
    background: #000;
    min-width: 800px;
    margin: 0;
    padding: 0;
    font: 13px Arial,Helvetica,sans-serif;
}
```

The author of Zen sometimes uses multiple definitions for one selector. For example, the body tag is defined in three places in `zen/style.css`. This approach to CSS allows you to organize things functionally and is preferred by some developers. Other people prefer to keep all the attributes of a specific selector together in one definition. In this text, we will use the latter approach, because it helps eliminate the need to go through extra steps required to manage the CSS inheritance issues. Accordingly, whenever I create a new selector in our `tao-fixed/style.css` file, I always have to go back through the other style sheets to eliminate (or comment out) any other definitions of the same style.

Now, let's add some more specifics to our primary div, page:

```
#page {
  width: 980px;
  margin: 0 auto;
  border-left: 4px solid #666633;
  border-right: 4px solid #666633;
  font-family: Arial, Helvetica, sans-serif;
  color: #111;
  line-height: 1.4em;
  background-color: #fff;
}
```

The definitions above cover the body text and set the tone for our theme's fontography. Now, let's add various other styles to cover more specialized text, like links and titles:

```
a, a:link, a:visited {
  color: #666633;
  text-decoration: none;
}

a:hover, a:focus {
  text-decoration: underline;
}

h1.title, h1.title a, h1.title a:hover {
  font-family: Verdana, Arial, Helvetica, sans-serif;
  font-weight: normal;
  color: #666633;
  font-size: 200%;
  margin: 0;
  line-height: normal;
}

h1, h1 a, h1 a:hover {
  font-size: 140%;
  color: #444;
  font-family: Verdana, Arial, Helvetica, sans-serif;
  margin: 0.5em 0;
}

h2, h2 a, h2 a:hover, .block h3, .block h3 a {
  font-size: 122%;
  color: #444;
```

```
    font-family: Verdana, Arial, Helvetica, sans-serif;
    margin: 0.5em 0;
}


h3 {
    font-size: 107%;
}


h3, h4, h5, h6 {
    font-weight: bold;
    font-family: Verdana, Arial, Helvetica, sans-serif;
}

#logo-title {
    margin: 10px 0 0 0;
    position: relative;
    background-color: #eaebcd;
    height: 60px;
    border-top: 1px solid #676734;
    padding-top: 10px;
    padding-bottom: 10px;
    border-bottom: 1px solid #676734;
}

#site-name a, #site-name a:hover {
    font-family: Verdana, Arial, Verdana, Sans-serif;
    font-weight: normal;
    color: #000;
    font-size: 176%;
    margin-left: 20px;
    padding: 0;
}

#site-slogan {
    color: #676734;
    margin: 0;
    font-size: 90%;
    margin-left: 20px;
}
```

Remember to go back and comment out any competing definitions in the other style sheets!

Formatting the Sidebars and Footer

The Left Sidebar is unused in this theme, but the Right Sidebar Region is essential, as it contains the main navigation and several Blocks. The way the CSS is written, the style definitions for Left and Right Sidebar are combined; we'll maintain that for convenience.

```css
#sidebar-left .block, #sidebar-right .block {
  padding-bottom: 15px;
  margin-bottom: 20px;
}
```

I want to control the styling of the menu in the Right Sidebar (our Navigation menu), so I will add the following:

```css
#sidebar-right ul.menu {
  border-top: 1px solid #676734;
  padding-top: 10px;
  padding-bottom: 10px;
  border-bottom: 1px solid #676734;
  background-color: #eaebcd;
  color: #676734;
  font-weight: normal;
  font-family: Verdana;
  line-height: 1.4em;
}

#sidebar-right ul.menu li {
  font-size: 110%;
  font-weight: normal;
}
```

The titles of the Blocks in the sidebar are controlled by the h2 tag. Let's add a definition for the h2 tags that appear inside this specific region:

```css
#sidebar-right h2 {
  background-color: #676734;
  display: block;
  color: #eaebcd;
  font-size: 110%;
  font-weight: normal;
  font-family: Verdana;
  line-height: 1.5em;
  padding-left: 10px;
}
```

I want the footer in this theme to anchor the page and to mirror the look and feel of the Page Top region we created earlier. The Footer region is wrapped with a `div` of the same name, so I need to modify `#footer` in my style sheet, as follows:

```
#footer-wrapper {
margin: 0;
}

#footer {
background-color: #676734;
color: #FFF;
margin: 0;
font-size: 100%;
height: 25px;
}

#footer a {
color: #fff;
}
```

I do not want to use a hover state for the footer links, so I will need to delete (or comment out) the definition `#footer a:hover` from the `tao/styles.css` file.

Formatting the Menus

In this theme, I want to employ horizontal menus for the top and bottom navigation menus; I also want to move the main navigation to the right column and make sure its style matches the rest of the site.

Creating the Horizontal Menu

First, let's set up horizontal presentation for the Primary Links menu, which appears at the top of the page. I want the links to appear in a horizontal line, aligned to the right:

```
#page-top li {
   display: inline;
   float: right;
}

#page-top li a {
   color: #fff;
}
```

Next, let's do the same for the navigation inside the Footer region, again, with right alignment:

```
#footer li {
  display: inline;
  float: right;
}
```

Formatting the Vertical Menu

Zen uses colored bullets for the navigation menu. The bullets are actually small image files and are contained in the `images` directory. The colors of the Zen bullets don't work well with the Tao color scheme, so I am going to apply a different style for the bulleted lists in the vertical menu.

All the styles relating to icons and bullets are in the `icons.css` file. Let's just eliminate the references to the images. Open the `icons.css` file and eliminate or comment out the following selectors:

- `.block li.leaf`
- `ul.menu li.leaf`
- `.block li.expanded`
- `ul.menu li.expanded`
- `.block ul li`

Now, let's modify one other style from this file. Copy the following code:

```
#main .node div.links {
  padding: 5px 0 5px 13px;
  background: url(images/links.gif) no-repeat 0 .93em;
}
```

into our `tao-fixed/style.css` file, and modify as follows:

```
#main .node div.links {
  padding: 5px 0 5px 13px;
}
```

Delete or comment out the original from the `icons.css` file, and save the file.

Formatting the Search Box

The search box formatting needs to be modified to match our new color scheme.

```
#search {
  position: absolute;
  padding: 0;
```

```
    top: 20px;
    right: 20px;
}

#search .form-text, #user-login-form .form-text {
    color: #444;
    border: 1px solid #000;
    padding: 2px;
}

#search .button,
#search .form-submit,
#user-login-form .button,
#user-login-form .form-submit {
    background-color: #676734;
    color: #fff;
    font-weight: bold;
    border: 1px solid #000;
}
```

Formatting the Comments Form and Output

We enabled the Comments functionality earlier, let's now set the look and feel. The Comments in the default Zen theme are shaded a light blue, consistent with the Zen color scheme. For Tao, we want to make things a little more conservative, a little more somber, so we will change that to a light gray and also apply our font selections.

Make the following changes to the selectors, below:

```
.comment {
    margin: 0 0 10px 0;
    padding: 10px;
    background: #f1f1f1;
}

.comment h3.title, .comment h3.title a {
    font-size: 122%;
    color: #666;
    font-weight: normal;
    font-family: Verdana, Arial, Sans-serif;
    margin-bottom: 3px;
    margin-top: 0;
}

.comment .new {
    color: #FFC600;
    font-weight: bold;
    font-family: Arial, Verdana, Sans-serif;
}
```

If what you see on your screen at this point is not largely similar to the image at the end of the chapter, odds are you have missed commenting out a selector; go back and check the style sheets in the `tao/` directory to make sure you deleted or commented out the proper selectors.

Adapting the Themeable Functions

We don't really need to make a large number of changes to our themeable functions to achieve our goals, but we will make some minor modifications to bring more consistency to the new look and feel.

Modifying template.php

First, let's look at the breadcrumb function that we inherited from the Zen theme:

```
function tao_breadcrumb($breadcrumb) {
    if (!empty($breadcrumb)) {
      return '<div class="breadcrumb">'. implode(' :: ', $breadcrumb)
.'</div>';
    }
}
```

I want to change the divider between the items in the breadcrumb trail from a double colon "::" to a double right arrow ">>", so we modify the function as follows:

```
function tao_breadcrumb($breadcrumb) {
    if (!empty($breadcrumb)) {
      return '<div class="breadcrumb">'. implode(' >> ', $breadcrumb)
.'</div>';
    }
}
```

Creating a New Template File

Our new theme Tao-Fixed is intended as a blog theme, so let's look at adjusting the formatting of the blog node. To do this, we are going to create a template file to control the output of the blog node; a template file is more specific, and hence preferred over the default node.tpl.php.

First, duplicate the file phptemplate/node.tpl.php (not the node.tpl.php file located in the tao/ directory!) and re-name it node-blog.tpl.php; this file will now be used by the system to handle the formatting of the blog node in our theme.

The following variables are available in the node.tpl.php file:

Variable	Purpose
$content	Node content, teaser if it is a summary.
$date	Formatted creation date.
$directory	The directory where the theme is located.
$id	The sequential ID of the node being displayed in a list.
$is_front	True if the front page is currently being displayed.
$links	Node links.
$name	Name of author.
$node	The node object.
$node_url	Link to node.
$page	True if the node is being displayed by itself as a page.
$picture	HTML for user picture.
$sticky	True if the node is sticky.
$submitted	Author and creation date information.
$taxonomy	Array of HTML links for taxonomy terms.
$teaser	Only returns the teaser rather than the full node text.
$terms	HTML for taxonomy terms.
$title	Title of node.
$zebra	Alternates between odd/even in a list.

The default file does not use all these variables, but that doesn't stop us from adding them in. Let's modify and format the information relating to the author and time of posting by modifying the code and adding the $date variable.

PHPTemplate Variables

Information on the various variables available in PHPTemplate can be found on Drupal.org and in Chapter 6 of this book:

`block.tpl.php`	`http://drupal.org/node/11813`
`box.tpl.php`	`http://drupal.org/node/11814`
`comment.tpl.php`	`http://drupal.org/node/11815`
`node.tpl.php`	`http://drupal.org/node/11816`
`page.tpl.php`	`http://drupal.org/node/11812`

Tao-Fixed is intended as a personal blog theme, so there's no need for us to display the author name — just the date will do fine. I also want to break away from the standard Drupal "submitted by" language and go with something simple, like simply stating "posted" followed by the date. To achieve this, I am going to eliminate `$submitted` for our template file and instead add my preferred language ("posted") and `$date`. I will also format the `$date` output to make it stand out a bit more.

The original statement looked like this:

```
<?php if ($submitted): ?>
    <span class="submitted"><?php print $submitted ?></span>
<?php endif; ?>
```

I am going to modify it as follows:

```
<?php if ($submitted): ?>
    <span class="submitted"><?php print t('Posted ') ?><strong><?php
print $date ?></strong></span>
<?php endif; ?>
```

I am also going to add the class `title` to the `$title` to gain more formatting control over this item, which by default was simply bracketed by an h2 tag.

The original statement looked like this:

```
<?php if ($page == 0): ?>
  <h2><a href="<?php print $node_url ?>" title="<?php print $title
?>"><?php print $title ?></a></h2>
<?php endif; ?>
```

I am going to modify it as follows:

```php
<?php if ($page == 0): ?>
  <h2 class="title"><a href="<?php print $node_url ?>" title="<?php
print $title ?>"><?php print $title ?></a></h2>
<?php endif; ?>
```

Save your file and you're done with this final step.

Before and After

When we started this process, we had the Zen-Fixed theme in place:

Now, after completing the changes to the CSS and themeable functions, we have Tao-Fixed:

Summary

This chapter showed intercepts and overrides in action. We went from a basic theme design, to a more specialized variation of the theme with a new look and feel. We made the conversion in three steps: Theme configuration, CSS modifications, and Themeable Function modifications.

Drupal's consistent usage of orders of precedence and the ability to leverage cascades of style sheets are keys to the success of this approach to theme creation. The ability to intercept and override the styles and the themeable functions made it possible for us to start with one design and end with a very different one—without having to code from scratch.

7
Building a New Theme

This chapter takes us into the world of building Drupal themes from scratch. While many people may begin their theme project by copying and modifying an existing theme, in this chapter, we cater to the purists who want to do it all themselves.

Inside we'll cover the basics of creating a new theme employing the PHPTemplate engine, and step through the various tasks required to produce a fully functional theme. In the last half of the chapter, we cover some of the more advanced techniques, including working with theme variables, employing multiple templates, and dynamic theming.

We close this chapter with a brief look at creating a pure PHP template, that is, theming Drupal without the use of a theme engine.

To follow fully the examples in this chapter, you will need your favorite web editor (Dreamweaver or another similar program) and, preferably, access to a development server on which to preview your work. In the section dealing with pure PHP themes, we will be using as our example the Chameleon theme from the default Drupal distro.

Planning the Build

How you go about building a theme is largely framed by your intentions for the theme. If you intend to release the theme for the use of others, then it is best to follow certain (albeit largely unwritten) conventions that make the resulting theme more "standard" and therefore, easier for others to use. In contrast, if use by others is not a factor, then you can proceed in a fashion that tailors the code more narrowly to your needs.

For purposes of our discussion in this chapter, I am going to assume you wish others to be able to use your theme and accordingly, our examples will tend toward standardization and increased flexibility without unnecessary complexity; this approach has the added advantage of decreasing your maintenance load going forward, and being more portable.

In terms of features, our goal here is to create a theme with the following attributes:

- Employs PHPTemplate
- Valid XHTML, pure CSS
- Supports one to three columns
- Supports theme configuration options native to PHPTemplate (e.g., logo, search box, site slogan, etc.)

Represented visually, the structure of our `page.tpl.php` file will be as follows:

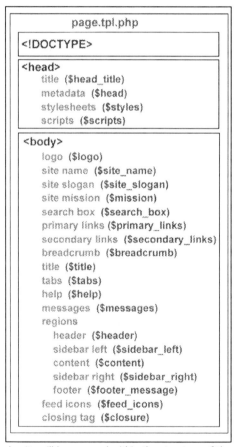

How the functional units will be grouped within the structure of the page.tpl.php file.

In terms of the layout that we will impose on the functionality, we will set up a standard three-column layout with a header and a footer, and then create the following structure to hold our functionality:

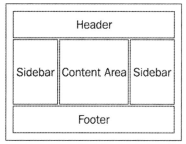

The general page layout we will define with the CSS for this theme

Regions are the primary key to placement of content and the functionality. By default, PHPTemplate provides for the following Regions:

- Header
- Content
- Sidebar Left
- Sidebar Right
- Footer

As discussed in previous chapters, you are not restricted to the default Regions. You can use all or only some of the Regions and you can also define new Regions if you so desire. For the example in this chapter, we will employ all the default Regions. If you are designing themes for others, it is best to include all the default Regions, as the system will show all the default Regions as options in the Block manager, regardless of whether they are present in the `page.tpl.php` file. Given the system's default display of these Regions in the Block manager, failing to include all the default Regions in your theme may lead to confusion for the site administrator.

 Adding new Regions is discussed in Chapter 5.

Now let's put this all together—here's a graphical representation of how our new theme will place the functional elements, including the Regions, relative to the CSS page divisions.

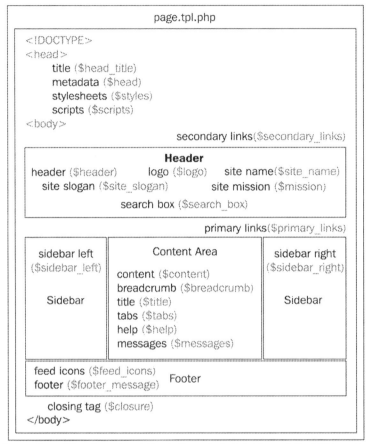

Diagram of the position of the elements relative to the principal divisions of the CSS layout and the main document divisions. Note that the ordering of the elements within the CSS is done alphabetically here, as the final ordering of the elements will be up to the individual developer.

Build a New PHPTemplate Theme

To create a new PHPTemplate-powered theme, we need to create the following files:

- `page.tpl.php`
- `style.css`

We'll also need a directory to hold them, so create a new directory and name it `Bluewater`; this will be the home directory—and the name—of our new theme.

Testing during theme development is easiest if you have access to a development server. Unlike straight HTML, it is difficult to preview the PHP files. If you have access to a development server, go ahead and place the Bluewater directory into the `sites/all/themes` directory. Next, copy into that directory a sample logo file we can work with and name it `logo.png`—the default Drupal logo used in the themes included in the distro will work just fine.

You can grab a copy from any of the default themes in the distro. Typically, the logo can be found inside the theme directory and is named `logo.png`, for example, `themes/garland/logo.png`.

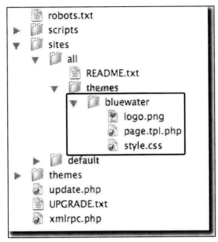

Place the directory and basic files for our new theme, Bluewater, inside `sites/all/themes`.

Building a page.tpl.php File

The `page.tpl.php` file is the key to creating a PHPTemplate theme. This essential file handles the placement of all the major page elements and the final HTML output. Accordingly, we will place in this file a mix of HTML and PHP. The PHP supplies the logic and the functionality, and the HTML supplies the formatting.

Take note of the ordering of the tags and the relationship between the PHP and the HTML. In this theme, we will typically place the HTML formatting inside the PHP conditional statements, rather than wrapping the PHP with HTML.

For example, we will typically want to order the tags like this (HTML inside the PHP):

```
<?php if ($site_slogan): ?>
  <div class="slogan">
  <?php print $site_slogan; ?>
  </div>
<?php endif; ?>
```

We generally don't want to do it like this (PHP inside the HTML):

```
<div class="slogan">
<?php if ($site_slogan): ?>
    <?php print $site_slogan; ?>
<?php endif; ?>
</div>
```

The reasoning behind the preference for the first ordering of tags is quite simple: if we place the HTML outside the PHP, then the appearance of the HTML will occur even when the condition contained in the PHP statement is not true, thereby clogging our page with unnecessary code and more importantly, creating unnecessary complexities in dealing with the styling of the page as a whole.

Again by way of example, compare the impact of the different orderings on the resulting source code. First, let's look at what happens when the HTML is placed inside the PHP.

Here's the source code with the **site slogan** functionality enabled by the administrator:

```
<!-- slogan -->
<div id="slogan">
this is the slogan
</div>
```

Compare that with the source code that results when the **site slogan** function is disabled:

```
<!-- slogan -->
```

In this case, the PHP conditional statement is false (**site slogan** disabled by the administrator) and, as a result, neither the **site slogan** nor its accompanying HTML formatting is displayed; the only thing that remains in the resulting source code is the comment tag.

Now, let's compare the source code that is produced when the PHP is wrapped with the HTML.

With **site slogan** enabled, you will see no difference:

```
<!-- slogan -->
<div id="slogan">
this is the slogan
</div>
```

But, when the **site slogan is** disabled, you do see a difference:

```
<!-- slogan -->
<div id="slogan">
</div>
```

In the latter example, the HTML is visible even though the conditional statement is false. The formatting remains despite the fact that the element the HTML is intended to format is not present. With this ordering of tags, we're always stuck with the presence of styles in the resulting code, regardless of whether the function it is supposed to format appears or not.

The example above makes another point as well, that is, how the use of the PHP conditional statements delivers benefits at run time. With the conditional statements in place, unneeded code is removed at run time. Without the conditional statements, the code remains for the browser to render, regardless of whether it is needed.

As a result of the interaction between the PHP conditional statements and the HTML tags, you will need to make decisions about whether you wish the styles to remain active in the absence of the element that the styling is intended to affect. In some cases, your layout integrity is maintained better by leaving the styling in place, regardless of whether the underlying element is active. In other cases, you will want the formatting to fold away when the element is not active—for example, a sidebar that collapses when no Blocks are assigned to a Region—and will therefore, want to use the PHP to control the visibility of the HTML.

 For a discussion of theme coding conventions, see the Drupal Theme Handbook at http://drupal.org/node/1965.

With that background behind us, let's create a new file, name it page.tpl.php, and get started on the code for our new theme.

Insert DocType and Head

Start by declaring the appropriate DocType. XHTML Strict is appropriate for this usage:

```
<!DOCTYPE html PUBLIC "-//W3C//DTD XHTML 1.0 Strict//EN" "http://www.
w3.org/TR/xhtml1/DTD/xhtml1-strict.dtd">
```

Next, place the opening HTML tag and name space. Note that this code also includes the PHP statements that call the appropriate language settings for your site, and should not be altered.

```
<html xmlns="http://www.w3.org/1999/xhtml" lang="<?php print $language
?>" xml:lang="<?php print $language ?>">
```

As the opening tag is an HTML declaration, go ahead and add the closing HTML tag now.

```
</html>
```

The rest of the code, discussed below, will be placed inside these two HTML tags.

Next, let's set up the head of the document. The various statements that compose the head of the document, including the metadata, the links to the style sheets, and any scripts, are produced by the following lines of code:

```
<head>
   <title>
       <?php print $head_title; ?>
   </title>
   <?php print $head; ?>
   <?php print $styles; ?>
   <?php print $scripts; ?>
</head>
```

Here,

- `$head_title` produces the site (not the page) title.
- `$head` includes the Drupal head code.
- `$styles` includes the various stylesheets.
- `$scripts` includes any necessary scripts.

There is no need to alter any of these, unless you have special needs (e.g., excluding the default Drupal style sheets).

Note that due to a quirk in the Internet Explorer browser, you may wish to add an empty `<script>` tag to your document head, e.g., `<script type="text/javascript"></script>`.

For more on this phenomenon visit `http://www.bluerobot.com/web/css/fouc.asp/`.

Insert Body Tags

Immediately after the `</head>` tag, open the `<body>` tag:

```
<body>
```

Then add a closing `</body>` tag:

```
</body>
```

All the code discussed in the section below will be placed inside the body tag.

Taken together, at this stage, you should now have the template's bare skeleton, like this:

```
<!DOCTYPE html PUBLIC "-//W3C//DTD XHTML 1.0 Strict//EN" "http://www.
w3.org/TR/xhtml1/DTD/xhtml1-strict.dtd">
<html xmlns="http://www.w3.org/1999/xhtml" lang="<?php print $language
?>" xml:lang="<?php print $language ?>">
<head>
  <title>
    <?php print $head_title; ?>
  </title>
  <?php print $head; ?>
  <?php print $styles; ?>
  <?php print $scripts; ?>
  <script type="text/javascript"> </script>
</head>
<body>
</body>
</html>
```

Into this document outline, we will now place the basic HTML that defines the layout of the output on the page. Once we have the basic HTML in place, we will insert the functional elements into the appropriate areas.

Lay Out the Page Divisions

The next step is to outline the general divisions that will define the layout of the page.tpl.php output. Between the <body> tags, add the following:

```
<div id="page-wrapper">
  <div id="header-wrapper">
    <div id="header-region">
    </div>
  </div>
  <div id="primary-links">
  </div>
  <div id="main-wrapper">
    <div id="sidebar-left-region">
    </div>
    <div id="content-region-<?php print $layout ?>">
    </div>
    <div id="sidebar-right-region">
    </div>
  </div>
  <div id="footer-region">
  </div>
</div>
```

Before we get started with placing the functional flesh on this HTML formatting skeleton, note that the organization of divs, above, wraps the entire body section inside <div id="page-wrapper">. Within that primary div, we create separate styling for the header, the primary links, the main content area, and finally, the footer. We have also set up dedicated styling for each of the five Regions — all nested inside the primary div.

Now, let's look at this in more detail as we add the functionality.

> Note the selector <div id="content-region-<?php print
> $layout ?>">. The use of the PHP statement inside the selector is
> discussed in detail later in this chapter, under the heading
> *Creating Dynamic CSS Styling*.

Place the Functional Elements

With our framework in place, we can now go back and place the functional elements where we want them to appear inside the layout.

Insert the Secondary Links

For this theme, I have placed the secondary links at the very top right-hand side of the page, before the header area. The placement is a subjective decision and here, instead of treating the secondary links as subnavigation to the primary links (which some templates do), I have separated them from the primary links, in order to create a second distinct area in which navigation can be positioned.

Here, the **secondary links** ($secondary_links), are placed with a conditional statement that allows this area of the layout to compress and disappear from view if the secondary links are not enabled.

```
<!-- secondary links -->
<?php if ($secondary_links): ?>
   <div id="secondary-links">
   <?php print theme('menu_links', $secondary_links); ?>
   </div>
<?php endif; ?>
```

Inside the Header Wrapper

The first section of our page layout is designated Header. Inside this page division, which will appear at the top of our final page, we will place a number of elements related to the site's identity as well as some basic functionality.

Logo

The following snippet includes the logo ($logo), with a hyperlink to the homepage. Note that the `title` and `alt` attributes are set by the code below. In this snippet, the image attributes are set to 'Click to return to the Homepage', but you can change this to whatever wording you wish. Note also the t function, which enables the translation feature of Drupal.

Wrap the logo inside a `div` with the id `logo`. In this case, I have placed the `div` outside the PHP. By wrapping the PHP with the styling, instead of placing the styling inside the conditional statement, we maintain the integrity of the size of the header area of our layout; we want this area of the layout to be stable and not changing size in response to the logo settings.

```
<!-- logo -->
<div id="logo">
   <?php if ($logo): ?>
   <a href="<?php print $base_path; ?>" title="<?php print t('Click to
return to the Homepage'); ?>">
<img src="<?php print $logo; ?>" alt="<?php print t('Click to return
to the Homepage '); ?>" /></a>
   <?php endif; ?>
</div>
```

The logo code in the example calls the system default logo image. The logo setting is controlled by the administrator in the theme and global configuration settings. If you intend to distribute your theme to others, you must place a logo file in the proper location (inside the directory), with the proper name (i.e., `logo.png`) and include it with your theme files. The Drupal logo is commonly used for this purpose.

Site Name

To include the **site name** (`$site_name`) on the page, together with a hyperlink to the homepage, add the code below. The `title` attribute of the `a` tag is set dynamically and tied to the translate functions (`t`). You can change the text from "Home" to whatever you wish.

A `div` named `sitename` is used to wrap the functionality. Unlike the logo, previously, the formatting here is inside the PHP conditional statement, so that the formatting is disabled if the **site name** is disabled.

```
<!-- site name -->
   <?php if ($site_name): ?>
     <div id="sitename">
        <h1><a href="<?php print $base_path ?>" title="<?php print
t('Home') ?>"><?php print $site_name; ?></a></h1>
     </div>
   <?php endif; ?>
```

Theme Search Box

The theme **search box** is inserted with the following snippet. Wrap this in a `div` with the `id searchbox`.

```
<!-- theme search box -->
<?php if ($search_box): ?>
   <div id="searchbox">
      <?php print $search_box; ?>
   </div>
<?php endif; ?>
```

Site Slogan

Here's the **site slogan** wrapped with a `div` with the `id site-slogan`:

```
<!-- slogan -->
<?php if ($site_slogan): ?>
   <div id="site-slogan">
      <?php print $site_slogan; ?>
   </div>
<?php endif; ?>
```

Site Mission

The **site mission** statement is included with $mission. Wrap it in a div with
the id mission:

```
<!-- mission statement -->
<?php if ($mission): ?>
    <div id="mission">
        <?php print $mission; ?>
    </div>
<?php endif; ?>
```

Header Region

Despite the confusing name, this has nothing to do with the header of the HTML
page — this is the Region used for the placement of blocks.

$header prints the Region to the page. Note that this employs a conditional statement
allowing the space for the Region to compress if nothing is assigned to the Region.

I have wrapped the Region with a div. The id here is header-region.

```
<!-- Region: header -->
<?php if ($header): ?>
    <div id="header-region">
        <?php print $header; ?>
    </div>
<?php endif; ?>
</div>
```

Insert the Primary Links

I am going to place the primary links in the space between the header wrapper and
the main wrapper. In this fashion, it is easy for me to control the formatting of this
area, which will span the width of the design.

The **primary links** for the site are included by the following. Note that the div is
inside the conditional statement so if the user decides not to use the primary links,
then the area compresses and is hidden from sight.

```
<?php if ($primary_links): ?>
    <div id="primary-links">
        <?php print theme('menu_links', $primary_links); ?>
    </div>
<?php endif; ?>
```

 The theme() code is used to automatically style the primary links. If you
want to modify this (beyond merely the CSS), take a look at the function
theme_menu_links for more information.

Inside the Main Wrapper

There is a bit more styling involved here, given that three columns and a wide range of functionality will be included in this critical area of the page. For this theme, in addition to the main content Region, we're placing the breadcrumb trail, title, tabs, help, messages, and feed icons inside the area between the two sidebars. To control all this, we will wrap the entire set of tags with one div (with the id main-content-wrapper), and then create formatting inside of that for each column and its constituent elements.

Sidebar Left

Let's place first the left sidebar ($sidebar_left), using a conditional statement to wrap the entire thing. We want this to compress and fold up if nothing is assigned to this Region, thereby allowing us to create a one- or two-column layout. Note the div controlling this Region has been named sidebar-left-region.

```php
<?php if ($sidebar_left): ?>
<div id="sidebar-left-region">
<?php print $sidebar_left; ?>
</div>
<?php endif; ?>
```

The Main Content Area

For the main content area of this design, I've created a div with a dynamic id. The div is used to wrap all the following elements. In a three-column layout, the area inside this div would be the center column. Regardless of how many columns are used, this area will hold the main content of the site by default.

Breadcrumb Trail

The breadcrumb functionality is placed on the screen with $breadcrumb. Note that while you can style this from within the page.tpl.php file, the creation of the breadcrumb trail is controlled by a themeable function. You can obtain the best control over the display and formatting settings by overriding the themeable function, rather than by styling this PHP statement.

```php
<!-- breadcrumb trail -->
<?php if ($breadcrumb): ?>
    <?php print $breadcrumb; ?>
<?php endif; ?>
```

 A list of all the themeable functions is included in Chapter 4.

Title

Insert the following conditional statement to place the page title on the screen. Style the title with the H2 tag and a dedicated class, content-title.

```
<!-- title -->
<?php if ($title): ?>
    <h2 class="content-title">
        ?php print $title; ?>
    </h2>
<?php endif; ?>
```

Tabs

$tabs controls the placement of the tabs-based navigation. Note that while the default front-end settings do not employ tabs, the default administration interface does; omitting this can cause you problems in the administration interface. Wrap the PHP print statement with a div and a class, tabs.

```
<!-- tabs -->
<?php if ($tabs): ?>
    <div class="tabs">
        <?php print $tabs; ?>
    </div>
<?php endif; ?>
```

Help

$help controls the output of the context-sensitive help information. The help link typically only appears in the admin interface. Note that you can style this statement if you choose. In this example, I have added no extra styling and left it to the system to provide the default styling.

```
<!-- help -->
<?php print $help; ?>
```

Messages

Insert $messages wherever you wish the system status and alerts messages to appear on your page. Note that you can style this statement if you choose. In this example, I have added no extra styling and left it to the system to provide the default styling.

```
<!-- messages -->
<?php print $messages; ?>
```

Content Region

The content Region ($content) is the primary Region used by the Drupal system to hold a variety of information, including nodes, the administration interface, and more. There is no conditional statement attached to this Region, because the system does not give the user the option to omit output to this Region. The formatting for this is covered by the div we've used to wrap the entire column; in our example, no additional styling is needed.

```
<!-- Region: content -->
<?php print $content; ?>
</div>
```

Sidebar Right

Let's close out this section of our page layout by including the right sidebar ($sidebar_right). Wrap this with a conditional statement so it will compress out of sight in the event nothing is assigned to the right sidebar. The div sidebar-right-Region is used to wrap the Region itself.

```
<?php if ($sidebar_right): ?>
    <div id="sidebar-right-region">
        <?php print $sidebar_right; ?>
    </div>
<?php endif; ?>
```

Inside the Footer

Last, at the bottom of our layout, is the footer Region. Let's wrap this with a div and name it appropriately. Inside the div, we will place the feed icons and the **footer message**.

```
<div id="footer-region">
```

Feed Icons

Place the RSS feed icon ($feed_icons) inside the div for the footer and wrap it in a div named feed-icons:

```
<!-- feed icons -->
<div id="feed-icons">
    <?php print $feed_icons; ?>
</div>
```

Footer Region

The Footer Region statement shows a variation in nomenclature — the string is named "footer_message" instead of simply "footer" (the latter would be more consistent with the names given to other Regions). The name, however, does not restrict the Region in any way. $footer_message provides both the footer Region and the output of the **footer message**, set by the administrator. Wrap $footer_message in a div so you can style it easily.

```
<!-- footer text -->
<div id="footer-text">
    <?php print $footer_message; ?>
</div>
</div>
```

 Note that as of Drupal 6, $footer_message is used only for placing the Footer Message (set in the site configuration by the administrator). The Footer Region will instead be controlled by $footer.

Insert the Template Closing Tag

A final snippet produces no output but is required by the Drupal system to close the logic of the template. Add this statement immediately before the closing body tag. No styling is needed.

```
<?php print $closure; ?>
```

The Final page.tpl.php File

At this stage, we've assembled all the necessary pieces of a fully functional PHPTemplate theme. All the elements you need are in place, though the styling is lacking. Let's stop here for a moment and get the Big Picture. Below is our raw page. tpl.php file, with only comment tags to enhance readability:

```
<!DOCTYPE html PUBLIC "-//W3C//DTD XHTML 1.0 Strict//EN" "http://www.
w3.org/TR/xhtml1/DTD/xhtml1-strict.dtd">
<html xmlns="http://www.w3.org/1999/xhtml" lang="<?php print $language
?>" xml:lang="<?php print $language ?>">
<head>
    <title>
        <?php print $head_title; ?>
    </title>
    <?php print $head; ?>
    <?php print $styles; ?>
    <?php print $scripts; ?>
```

```
    <script type="text/javascript"> </script>

</head>

<body>

<div id="page-wrapper">

    <!-- secondary links -->
        <?php if ($secondary_links): ?>
          <div id="secondary-links">
          <?php print theme('menu_links', $secondary_links); ?>
          </div>
        <?php endif; ?>

<!-- BEGIN Header -->
<div id="header-wrapper">

    <!-- logo -->
    <div id="logo">
        <?php if ($logo): ?>
            <a href="<?php print $base_path; ?>" title="<?php print
            t('Click to return to the Home page'); ?>"><img src="<?php
            print $logo; ?>" alt="<?php print t('Click to return to
            the Home page '); ?>" /></a>
        <?php endif; ?>
    </div>

    <!-- site name -->
        <?php if ($site_name): ?>
          <div id="sitename">
          <h1><a href="<?php print $base_path ?>" title="<?php print
          t('Home') ?>"><?php print $site_name; ?></a></h1>
          </div>
        <?php endif; ?>

    <!-- theme search box -->
        <?php if ($search_box): ?>
          <div id="searchbox">
          <?php print $search_box; ?>
          </div>
        <?php endif; ?>

    <!-- slogan -->
        <?php if ($site_slogan): ?>
          <div id="site-slogan">
          <?php print $site_slogan; ?>
          </div>
        <?php endif; ?>
```

```
<!-- site mission -->
    <?php if ($mission): ?>
       <div id="mission">
       <?php print $mission; ?>
       </div>
    <?php endif; ?>

    <!-- Region: header -->
    <?php if ($header): ?>
       <div id="header-region">
       <?php print $header; ?>
       </div>
    <?php endif; ?>

</div>

<!-- END Header -->

<!-- primary links -->
    <?php if ($primary_links): ?>
       <div id="primary-links">
       <?php print theme('menu_links', $primary_links); ?>
       </div>
    <?php endif; ?>

<!-- BEGIN Center Content -->
<div id="main-wrapper">

    <!-- Region: sidebar left -->
    <?php if ($sidebar_left): ?>
       <div id="sidebar-left-region">
       <?php print $sidebar_left; ?>
       </div>
    <?php endif; ?>

    <div id="content-region-<?php print $layout ?>">

       <!-- breadcrumb trail -->
       <?php if ($breadcrumb): ?>
          <?php print $breadcrumb; ?>
       <?php endif; ?>

       <!-- title -->
       <?php if ($title): ?>
          <h2 class="content-title"><?php print $title; ?></h2>
       <?php endif; ?>

       <!-- tabs -->
```

```php
            <?php if ($tabs): ?>
                <div class="tabs">
                <?php print $tabs; ?>
                </div>
            <?php endif; ?>

        <!-- help -->
            <?php print $help; ?>

        <!-- messages -->
            <?php print $messages; ?>

    <!-- Region: content -->
        <?php print $content; ?>

    </div>

    <!-- Region: sidebar right -->
        <?php if ($sidebar_right): ?>
            <div id="sidebar-right-region">
            <?php print $sidebar_right; ?>
            </div>
        <?php endif; ?>

</div>
<!-- END Content Area -->

<!-- BEGIN Footer -->
    <!-- Region: footer -->
        <div id="footer-region">

    <!-- feed icons -->
        <div id="feed-icons">
        <?php print $feed_icons; ?>
        </div>

    <!-- footer text -->
        <div id="footer-text">
        <?php print $footer_message; ?>
        </div>

</div>
<!-- END Footer -->

<!-- theme closing tag -->
    <?php print $closure; ?>

</div>
</body>
</html>
```

The style.css File

Let's go back now and open up the `style.css` file we created at the beginning of this chapter. Use this file to define the various selectors we've placed in the `page.tpl.php` file. In addition to the selectors we've used to control the placement of the functionality, you will need to define various tags, classes, and IDs to specify fonts and style the information hierarchy. You may also wish to add decorative touches via some creative CSS. All the theme-specific styles should be defined in this document, along with any overrides of existing selectors.

Because an exhaustive CSS tutorial is beyond the scope of this text, we're not going to go through all the various styling. The file is included, below, for your review:

```css
/** global styles **/
body {
    font: 13px/16px Verdana, Arial, Helvetica, sans-serif;
    color: #CCCCCC;
    background-color: #CCCCCC;
}

#page-wrapper {
    position:relative;
    width:974px;
    text-align:left;
    background-color: #336699;
    border: solid 12px #FFFFFF;
    margin-top: 0;
    margin-right: auto;
    margin-bottom: 0;
    margin-left: auto;
}

a, a:link, a:visited {
  color: #FFFFFF;
  text-decoration: none;
}

a:hover, a:focus {
  color: #6191C5;
  text-decoration: underline;
}

a:active, a.active {
  color: #89A3E4;
```

```
    }
h1.title, h1.title a, h1.title a:hover {
  font-family: "Trebuchet MS", Arial, Helvetica, sans-serif;
  font-weight: normal;
  color: #6191C5;
  font-size: 200%;
  margin:0;
  margin-bottom:0px;
  line-height:normal;
}

h1, h1 a, h1 a:hover {
  font: 20px/20px Arial, Helvetica, sans-serif;
  color: #FFFFFF;
  margin: 0;
}

h2,  h3 {
  font: 18px/18px Arial, Helvetica, sans-serif;
  color: #FFFFFF;
  margin: 2px 0 0 0;
  padding: 2px 5px;
  border: dashed 1px #FFFFFF;
}

h2 a, h2 a:hover, .block h3, .block h3 a {
  font: 18px/22x Arial, Helvetica, sans-serif;
  color: #FFFFFF !important;
  margin: 0;
  padding: 0;
}

#sidebar-left-region h2,
#sidebar-left-region h3,
#sidebar-right-region h2,
#sidebar-right-region h3 {
  font: 16px/16px Arial, Helvetica, sans-serif;
  color: #FFFFFF;
  margin: 0;
  padding: 20px 0 0 0;
  border: none;
  }
```

```
h4, h5, h6 {
  font-weight: bold;
  font-family: Arial, Helvetica, sans-serif;
}

/** header styles **/
#header-wrapper {
    position: relative;
    display: block;
    background-color: #336699;
    height: 120px;
}

#header-region {
}

#logo {
    float: left;
    width: 50px;
    margin: 12px 0 0 12px;
    padding: 8px 12px;
    border: solid 10px #FFFFFF;
    background-color: #6699CC;
}

#sitename {
    float: left;
    margin-top: 30px;
}

#sitename h1 a{
    font: 28px/28px Arial, "Century Gothic", Verdana;
    color: #FFFFFF;
    margin-left: 7px;
    text-decoration: none;
}

#searchbox {
    float:right;
    width:210px;
    height: 20px;
    margin-top:85px;
    margin-right:0px;
}
```

```
#search .form-text {
  width: 137px;
  vertical-align: middle;
  border: 1px solid #6699CC;
}

#search .form-submit {
  padding: 0 3px;
  vertical-align: middle;
  border-top: 1px solid #FFFFFF;
  border-right: 1px solid #666666;
  border-bottom: 1px solid #666666;
  border-left: 1px solid #FFFFFF;
}

.submitted {
  color: #333333;
}

.submitted a{
  color: #000000;
}

#primary-links {
    position: relative;
    display: block;
    height:20px;
    width:974px;
    border-top: solid 12px #FFFFFF;
    background-color: #666666;
}

#primary-links ul {
  padding:0;
  margin:0;
  list-style:none;
}

#primary-links ul li {
  display:inline;
}
```

```
#primary-links ul li a, #primary-links ul li a:visited {
  padding: 3px 10px 0 10px;
  font: 10px/13px Verdana, Arial, Helvetica, sans-serif;
  color: #FFFFFF;
  float: right;
}

#primary-links ul li a:hover {
  color: #000000;
}

#secondary-links {
    position: relative;
    display: block;
    height:20px;
    width:974px;
    margin-top: -12px;
    border-bottom: solid 12px #FFFFFF;
    background-color: #666666;
}

#secondary-links ul {
    list-style: none;
}

#secondary-links ul li {
    display: inline;
}

#secondary-links ul li a, #secondary-links ul li a:visited {
  padding: 3px 10px 0 10px;
  font: 10px/13px Verdana, Arial, Helvetica, sans-serif;
  color: #FFFFFF;
  float: right;
}

#secondary-links ul li a:hover {
  color: #000000;
}
#mission {
    position: absolute;
    left: 113px;
    top: 60px;
}
```

```
#site-slogan {
   position: absolute;
   left: 113px;
   top: 73px;
}

/** content area styles **/
#main-wrapper{
   position: relative;
   width:auto;
   height: 100%;
   border-top: solid 12px #FFFFFF;
   background-color: #336699;
}

#content-region-none {
   padding: 12px 10px 10px 10px;
   position: relative;
}

#content-region-left {
   width: 743px;
   padding:12px 0px 10px 10px;
   position: relative;
   float:left;
}

#content-region-right {
   width: 743px;
   padding:12px 10px 10px 10px;
   position: relative;
   float:left;
}

#content-region-both {
   width: 533px;
   padding:12px 10px 10px 10px;
   position: relative;
   float:left;
}

#tabs {
}
```

```
.content-title {

}

/** sidebar styles **/
#sidebar-left-region{
    position:relative;
    float:left;
    width:200px;
    padding: 0px 0 0 10px;
}

#sidebar-right-region{
    position:relative;
    float:right;
    width:200px;
    padding: 0px 10px 0 0;
}

/** footer styles **/
#footer-region {
    position:relative;
    width: auto;
    height:40px;
    margin:0 auto;
    clear:both;
    border-top:12px solid #FFFFFF;
}

#feed-icons {
    float:right;
    padding: 8px;
}

#footer-text {
    position:relative;
    display: block;
    height: 30px;
    float:left;
    color: #FFFFFF;
    font-size: 10px;
    line-height: 35px;
    left: 10px;
}
```

```css
/** Admin Style **/
/* Tabs */
ul.primary {

    border-bottom: solid 1px #18324B;
}

ul.secondary {

    border-bottom: solid 1px #18324B;
}

ul.primary li.active a.active {
    background-color:#2B5986;
    border: solid 1px #18324B;
}

ul.primary li a {
    background-color:#6699CC;
}

ul.secondary li  {
    margin-bottom: 5px;
}

/* Region: content */
#content-region-both table  {
    width: 530px;
}

table thead {
    color: #FFFFFF;
}
table tbody tr.odd,
table tbody tr.odd td.menu-disabled{
    background: #2B5986;
    border-bottom: solid 1px #336699;
}

table tbody tr.even,
table tbody tr.even td.menu-disabled{
    background: #2D5E8D;
    border-bottom: solid 1px #336699;
}
```

```
table tr td.region{
    font-weight: normal;
    color:#FFFFFF;
    background:  #6699CC;
}

ul.secondary li.active a.active {
    border-bottom: solid 1px #18324B;
}
```

 In addition to your theme-specific selectors, you may need to re-define the portions of the /modules/system/admin.css file that affect the administrator's interface.

While the vast majority of the selectors defined in our style.css are basic (we used a bare minimum for this example), you should note the following, which relate to the implementation of the three-column layout:

```
#content-region-none {
padding: 12px 10px 10px 10px;
position: relative;
}

#content-region-left {
width: 743px;
padding:12px 0px 10px 10px;
position: relative;
float: left;
}

#content-region-right {
width: 743px;
padding:12px 10px 10px 10px;
position: relative;
float: left;
}

#content-region-both {
width: 533px;
padding:12px 10px 10px 10px;
position: relative;
float: left;
}
```

These selectors work together with the dynamic styling we applied to the main content column (`<div id="content-region-<?php print $layout ?>">`) to create a center column that expands to fill either the right or left column when either of the sidebars carry no blocks. The styles, in other words, are critical to creating a template that can support a one-, two- or three-column layout.

The technique used to create the fluid columns structure is discussed below, in the section on *Creating Dynamic CSS Styling*.

A Look at Our New Theme

With the completion of the `style.css` file, the new theme is ready for use.

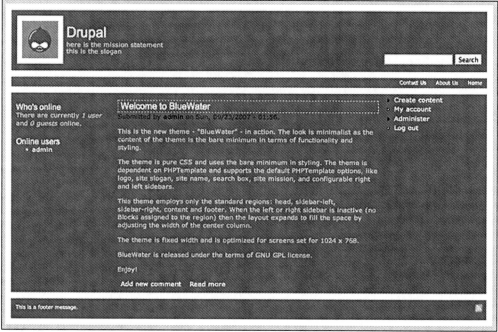

Our new theme in action. Note that this screenshot shows sample content and dummy text in position for testing the primary links, the main content area, the site slogan, site mission, and footer message. The Who's Online block has also been assigned to the Left Region.

If you wish to distribute your theme and share it with the Drupal community (something we strongly encourage!), you will need to include a thumbnail of the theme in action. Take note of Drupal's guidelines for theme screenshots, as they are rather specific http://drupal.org/node/11637.

Extending Your PHPTemplate Theme

Working with Template Variables

Drupal produces variables that can be used to enhance the functionality of themes. Typically, a function is placed in a template file. The function returns values reflecting the state of the template. A function may indicate, for example, whether the page is the front page of the site, or whether there are one, two, or three active columns. Tapping into this information is a convenient way for a theme developer to style a site dynamically.

The default Drupal variables cover the most common (and essential) functions, including creating unique identifiers for items. Some of the Drupal variables are unique to particular templates, others are common to all. In addition to the default variables, you can also define your own variables.

Let's look first at the default Drupal variables, then at intercepting and overriding the default variables, and finally, at creating your own variables.

Variables Available in block.tpl.php

The system provides the following variables for the `block.tpl.php` template:

The `$block` object includes the following standard fields:

Variable	Function
`$block->content`	The HTML content for the block.
`$block->delta`	The number of the block.
`$block->module`	The name of the module that generated the block.
`$block->region`	The Region name (can be any Region defined by system or user).
`$block->status`	The status of the block (either 0 or 1).
`$block->subject`	The block's title.
`$block->throttle`	The throttle setting.

Other variables available in the block template include:

Variable	Function
$block_id	Unique to the block.
$block_zebra	Odd/even label created for each block, unique to each sidebar.
$directory	The directory in which the theme is located.
$id	Sequential ID of the block (first block is 1; second block is 2, etc.).
$is_front	True if the front page is currently being displayed, false if not.
$zebra	Creates alternating label for blocks (odd or even).

A list of both current and superseded variables available for the block template is maintained at the official Drupal site at http://drupal.org/node/11813.

Variables Available in box.tpl.php

The system provides the following variables for the box.tpl.php template.

Variable	Function
$content	The content of the box.
$region	The name of the Region in which the box is displayed.
$title	The title of the box.

A list of both current and superseded variables available for the box template is maintained on the official Drupal site at http://drupal.org/node/11814.

Variables Available in comment.tpl.php

The system provides the following variables for the `comment.tpl.php` template.

Variable	Function
$author	Name of comment's author with a link to the author profile.
$comment (object)	The comment object.
$content	The body of the comment.
$date	Formatted creation date of the post.
$directory	The relative path to the directory in which the theme is located.
$id	Sequential ID of the comment displayed (first comment is 1, second comment is 2, etc.).
$is_front	True if the front page is currently being displayed, false if not.
$links	The links below the comment.
$new	Text for 'new' (where the comment is new).
$picture	HTML for user's picture.
$submitted	The **Submitted by** text.
$title	Link to the comment title.
$zebra	Creates alternating label for comments ('odd' and 'even').

 A list of both current and superseded variables available for the comment template is maintained on the official Drupal site at `http://drupal.org/node/11815`.

Variables Available in node.tpl.php

The system provides the following variables for the `node.tpl.php` template.

Variable	Function
$content	Node content (teaser if it is a summary).
$date	Formatted creation date of the node.
$directory	The relative path to the directory in which the theme is located.
$id	The sequential ID of the node displayed in a list.

Variable	Function
$is_front	True if the front page is currently being displayed, false if not.
$links	The links associated with the node (e.g., **read more, add comment**).
$name	The formatted name of the user who authored the page.
$node (object)	The node object.
$node_url	The permanent URL to the node.
$page	True if the node is being displayed by itself as a page.
$picture	HTML for user's picture.
$sticky	True if the node is sticky.
$submitted	The **Submitted by** text.
$taxonomy (array)	An array of HTML links for the taxonomy terms.
$teaser	Whether the teaser is displayed (true or false).
$terms	HTML for the taxonomy terms associated with this node.
$title	The title of the node.
$zebra	Creates alternating label for nodes ('odd' and 'even').

 A list of both current and superseded variables available for the node template is maintained on the official Drupal site at `http://drupal.org/node/11816`.

Variables Available in page.tpl.php

In additional to the basic variables included in the example `page.tpl.php` file we built earlier in this chapter, there are a number of other variables that are available for your use:

Variable	Function
$base_path	The base URL path of the Drupal installation.
$breadcrumb	HTML for displaying the breadcrumb trail.
$closure	Placed at bottom of page to provide closure for any dynamic JavaScripts that need to be called once the page has been displayed.
$content	The HTML content generated by Drupal.
$css	An array of all the CSS files for the page.
$directory	The relative path to the directory in which the theme is located.

Variable	Function
`$feed_icons`	The links to the RSS feeds for the page.
`$footer_message`	The footer, including the footer message set by the admin.
`$head`	The HTML that will appear inside the `<head></head>` tags.
`$head_title`	The text displayed in the page title (between the `<title>` and `</title>` tags).
`$help`	The dynamic help text.
`$is_front`	True if the front page is currently displayed, false if not.
`$language`	The site's language setting.
`$layout`	Set different types of layout, depending on how many sidebars are enabled (values include `none`, `left`, `right`, `both`).
`$logo`	Sets path to logo image (as defined in admin).
`$messages`	HTML for status and error messages.
`$mission`	The text of the **site mission**, as defined in admin.
`$node`	Available when displaying a node in full page view.
`$primary_links (array)`	An array containing the links designated as primary by admin.
`$scripts`	Loads the `<script>` tags into the page.
`$search_box`	The HTML for the theme search box.
`$secondary_links (array)`	An array containing the links designated as secondary by the admin.
`$sidebar_left`	The HTML for the left sidebar Region.
`$sidebar_right`	The HTML for the right sidebar Region.
`$site_name`	The **site name**, as defined by admin.
`$site_slogan`	The **site slogan**, as defined by admin.
`$styles`	Includes the style sheets.
`$tabs`	HTML for displaying the tabs.
`$title`	The main content title, typically the node title.

 A list of both current and superseded variables available for the page template is maintained on the official Drupal site at `http://drupal.org/node/11812`.

Intercepting and Overriding Variables

You can intercept and override the system's existing variables. Intercepting a variable is no different in practice from intercepting a themeable function: you simply restate it in the `template.php` file and make your modifications there, leaving the original code in the core intact. In this fashion, you are able to maintain your modifications inside the theme directory, rather than by modifying the core files.

 The basic principles behind intercepts and overrides are discussed at length in Chapter 4.

To intercept an existing variable and override it with your new variable, you need to use the function `_phptemplate_variables()`, which is added to the `template.php` file with the following syntax:

```php
<?php
function _phptemplate_variables($hook, $vars = array()) {
  switch ($hook) {
    // add your code here...
  }

  return $vars;
}
?>
```

Let's take an example and apply this. Assume you wish to substitute a new value for `$title` in `page.tpl.php`. To accomplish this task, add the following code to the `template.php` file:

```php
<?php
function _phptemplate_variables($hook, $vars = array()) {
    switch ($hook) {
        case 'page' :
            $vars['title'] = 'override title';
        break;
    }
    return $vars;
}
?>
```

With this change made and the file saved to your theme, the string "override title" will appear, substituted for the original `$title` value. Note that the function specifies `'page'`; this points our function to the page theme hook.

Making New Variables Available

PHPTemplate also allows you to define additional custom variables in your theme. To create a new variable, you must declare the function _phptemplate_variables() in the template.php file. The syntax is the same as that just used for intercepting and overriding a variable:

```php
<?php
function _phptemplate_variables($hook, $vars = array()) {
  switch ($hook) {
    // add your code here...
  }

  return $vars;
}
?>
```

In this case, we will add a new variable, 'newvar' to the page theme hook:

```php
<?php
function _phptemplate_variables($hook, $vars = array()) {
  switch ($hook) {
    case 'page' :
      $vars['newvar'] = 'new variable';
      break;
  }
  return $vars;
}
?>
```

The ability to add new variables to the system is a powerful tool and gives you the ability to add more complex logic to your template, for example, to set variables to track user status (logged in or not).

Dynamic Theming

The Drupal system, when combined with the PHPTemplate engine, gives you the ability to create logic that displays specific templates or specific elements automatically in response to the existence of certain conditions. We have in previous chapters seen some of this logic in action, for example, by inserting PHP code into a block to control the visibility of the block.

 See Chapter 2 for a discussion of controlling block visibility.

In this section, we take the discussion one step further and look at running multiple themes and creating dynamic elements and styles.

Using Multiple Templates

Most advanced sites built today employ multiple page templates. In this section, we will look at the most common scenarios and how to address them with a PHPTemplate theme.

 While there are many good reasons for running multiple page templates, you should not create additional templates solely for the purpose of disabling Regions to hide Blocks. While the approach will work, it will result in a performance hit for the site, as the system will still produce the Blocks, only to then wind up not displaying them for the pages. The better practice is to control your Block visibility using the techniques discussed in Chapter 2.

A Separate Admin Theme

With the arrival of Drupal 5, one of the most common Drupal user requests was satisfied; that is, the ability to easily designate a separate admin theme. Prior to Drupal 5, setting up a separate theme for the admin section had to be done manually — there was no admin shortcut. Since Drupal 5, however, it has been a simple matter that you can handle directly from the admin interface, without the need for additional coding.

To designate a separate theme for your admin section, follow these steps:

1. Log in and access your admin screen.
2. Go to **Site configuration**.
3. Access **Administration theme** and then select the theme you desire from the drop-down box, which lists all the installed themes.
4. Click **Save configuration**, and your selected theme should appear immediately.

 The installation of additional pre-configured themes is covered in Chapter 2 of this text.

Multiple Page or Section Templates

In contrast with the ease of setting up a separate administration template is the comparative difficulty of setting up multiple templates for different pages or sections.

The bad news is that you must manually configure the system to use separate templates for separate pages or sections. The good news is that it is possible to attain a high degree of granularity from PHPTemplate; you could literally define distinct templates for every page of a site, if you should so desire.

As discussed in Chapter 5, Drupal employs an order of precedence based on a naming convention. You can unlock the granularity of the system through proper application of the naming convention. It is possible, for example, to associate templates with every element on the path, or with specific users, or with a particular functionality, all through the simple process of creating a new template and naming it appropriately.

The system will search for alternative templates, preferring the specific to the general, and failing to find a more specific template, will apply the default `page.tpl.php`. Consider the following example of the order of precedence and the naming convention in action.

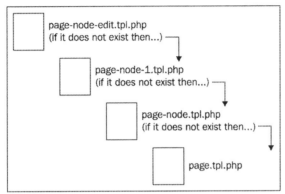

The custom templates above could be used to override the default page.tpl.php and theme either an entire node (page-node.tpl.php), or simply the node with an ID of 1 (page-node-1.tpl.php), or the node in edit mode (page-node-edit.tpl.php), depending on the name given the template.

In the example above, the page-node templates would be applied to the node in full page view. In contrast, should you wish to theme the node in its entirety, you would need to intercept and override the default `node.tpl.php`. See the discussion later in this chapter for more on this topic.

The fundamental methodology of the system is to use the first template file it finds and ignore other, more general templates (if any). This basic principle, combined with proper naming of the templates, gives you control over the template used in various situations.

Let's take a series of four examples to show how this feature can be used to provide solutions to common problems:

1. Creating a unique home page template
2. Using a different template for a group of pages
3. Assigning a specific template to a specific page
4. Designating a specific template for a specific user

Creating A Unique Homepage Template

Let's assume that you wish to set up a unique theme for the homepage of a site.

Employing separate themes for the homepage and the interior pages is one of the most common requests web developers hear. With Drupal, you can achieve some variety within a theme by controlling the visibility of blocks on the homepage, but sometimes that is not enough flexibility — you want to do more. If you need more options, you may wish to employ a completely separate template that is purpose-built for your homepage content.

The easiest way to set up a distinct front page template is to copy the existing `page.tpl.php` file, rename it, and make your changes to the new file. Alternatively, you can create a new file from scratch. In either situation, your front-page-specific theme must be named `page-front.tpl.php`. The system will automatically display your new file for the site's homepage, and use the default `page.tpl.php` for the rest of the site.

Using a Different Template for a Group of Pages

Next, let's associate a theme with a group of pages. You can theme any distinct group of pages, using as your guide the path for the pages. For example, to theme all the user pages (as opposed to the user page for just one user ID), you would create the template `page-user.tpl.php`.

To theme according to the type of content, you can associate your page template with a specific node, for example, all blog entry pages can be controlled by the file `page-blog-tpl.php`.

Assigning a Specific Template to a Specific Page

Taking this to its extreme, you can associate a specific template with a specific page. By way of example, assume we wish to provide a unique template for a specific content item. Our example page is located at `http://www.demosite.com/?q=node/2`; accordingly, we need to create a template with the following name: `page-node-2.tpl.php`.

A Note on Templates and URLs

Drupal bases the template order of precedence on the default path generated by the system. If the site is using a module, like pathauto, which alters the path that appears to site visitors, remember that your templates will still be searched based on the original paths.

The official Drupal community site provides examples of several ways you can add a variable to the `template.php` file to avoid this problem and provide support for URL aliases. Visit Drupal.org for a discussion of the various techniques at `http://drupal.org/node/117491`.

Designating a Specific Template for a Specific User

Assume that you want to add a personalized theme for the super administrator. To do this, copy the existing `page.tpl.php` file, rename it to reflect its association with the specific user, and make any changes to the new file. To associate the new theme file with the Super Administrator, name the template file: `page-user-1.tpl.php`.

Now, when user 1 logs into the site, they will be presented with this template. Only user 1 will see it and only when they are logged in and visiting their account pages.

Dynamically Theming Page Elements

In addition to being able to style particular pages or groups of pages, Drupal and PHPTemplate make it possible to provide specific styling for different page elements.

Associating Elements with the Front Page

Drupal provides `$is_front` as a means of determining whether the page currently displayed is the front page.

`$is_front` is set to true if Drupal is rendering the front page; otherwise it is set to false. We can use `$is_front` to help toggle display of items we want to associate with the front page.

To display an element on only the front page, make it conditional on the state of `$is_front`. For example, to display the **site mission** only on the front page, wrap `$mission` as follows:

```php
<?php if ($is_front): ?>
  <div id="mission">
  <?php print $mission; ?>
  </div>
<?php endif; ?>
```

To set up an alternative condition, so that one element will appear on the front page but a different element will appear on other pages, modify the statement like this:

```php
<?php if ($is_front): ?>
    //whatever you want to display on front page
<?php else: ?>
      //what is displayed when not on the front page
<?php endif; ?>
```

Dynamically Styling Modules and Blocks

In Chapter 5, we discussed at length the process of intercepting and overriding themeable functions. Those functions supply much of the key output on a Drupal site and many are positioned on the page through Blocks. In this chapter, we want to look at how to control the formatting of a site's Blocks, regardless of their contents.

Block output is controlled by the `block.tpl.php` template. As we have seen in other areas, PHPTemplate will look to the names given multiple template files to determine which template to display. The order of precedence used for the Block template is consistent with that used elsewhere:

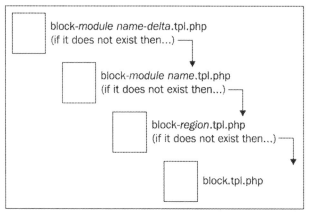

The naming convention determines what is displayed. At the most specific, you can provide a template to apply to the Blocks of a specific module of a specific delta (block-modulename-delta.tpl.php). You can also attach a template to Blocks of a module by module name (block-modulename.tpl.php), or to the Blocks of a particular Region (block-regionname.tpl.php). Failing the presence of any of the above, the system applies the default block.tpl.php template.

Note that the order of precedence includes the module name, that is, the name of the module that produces the output being displayed in the Block. Delta is a system-generated value that provides a unique identifier.

If you are not certain of the provenance of your Block, that is, the name of the module that produces it or its delta, try the following, which will give you information on all Blocks on a particular page:

1. Open your theme's `block.tpl.php` file (or create it if it does not exist).
2. Add the following at the top of the file:
   ```
   <pre>
   <?php print_r($block); ?>
   </pre>
   ```
3. Save.
4. Load the page in a browser.

When you view the page, the information will appear for each Block active on that page. Here's the information that would appear for our theme Bluewater, when the **Who's Online** Block is placed in the left sidebar:

```
stdClass Object
(
    [module] => user
    [delta] => 3
    [theme] => bluewater
    [status] => 1
    [weight] => 0
    [region] => left
    [custom] => 0
    [throttle] => 0
    [visibility] => 0
    [pages] =>
    [title] =>
    [subject] => Who's online
    [content] => There are currently...
```

Note we are given the name of the module that produces the output in this Block (User), the delta (3), as well as other information like the weight, the Region, etc.

With this information, we can then assemble the following example showing the order of precedence relative to this Block:

Template	Will apply to...
block-user-3.tpl.php	the Who's Online block
block-user.tpl.php	All blocks output by the User module
block-left.tpl.php	All blocks in the sidebar-left region
block.tpl.php	All blocks

Dynamically Styling Nodes

PHPTemplate provides a specific template for nodes — node.tpl.php. Using the same principles of precedence we've seen throughout, you can provide alternative node templates to suit your needs. To provide a template for the blog node, for example, create node-blog.tpl.php; for the story node, node-story.tpl.php. In the absence of a more specific template, the system will apply the default node. tpl.php file.

Creating Dynamic CSS Styling

Just as the system dynamically creates new IDs for nodes, you can easily add a similar functionality to your CSS selectors, enabling you to generate dynamic styling.

Using Dynamic Selectors for Nodes

As an alternative to creating unique node templates, you can provide a degree of individual node styling through the CSS. By default, the system generates a unique CSS ID for each node on the website. To create a node-specific selector to take advantage of this feature, use the following nomenclature for the ID:

```
#node-[nid] {
}
```

For example, assume you wish to add a border to the node with the ID of 2. Simply create a new `div` in `style.css` with the name:

```
#node-2 {
border: 1px solid #336600
}
```

Changing the Selector Based on $layout

One of the easiest modifications you can make is to make the selector responsive to the layout.

`$layout` is provided by the system to help enable this functionality. To make a class specific to the layout, add `$layout` to the class in the template file. For example, to make `class=content` reflect the layout in action, state the class as follows:

```
class="content-<?php print $layout ?>"
```

This code will result in variations on the class, `content-none`, `content-left`, `content-right`, `content-both`, with the appropriate selector being active depending on the presence of all, one, or none of the sidebars.

Column layout	$layout suffix
No sidebars	none
Left sidebar only	left
Right sidebar only	right
Both sidebars	both

`$layout` provides the key to easily creating collapsible sidebars. To set up this functionality, modify the primary container style to include `$layout`. In the example theme we created earlier in this chapter, we will modify this line of the `page.tpl.php` file from:

```
<div id="main-wrapper">
```

to:

```
<div id="main-wrapper-<?php print $layout ?>">
```

Now, go to the `style.css` file and define the following:

```
#main-wrapper-none {
}

#main-wrapper-left {
}

#main-wrapper-right {
}

#main-wrapper-both {
}
```

The final step is to create the styling for each of the selectors above.

When the site is viewed, the value of `$layout` will determine which selector is applied. You can now specify, through the selectors above, exactly how the page appears — whether the columns collapse, the resulting widths of the remaining columns, etc., etc.

 This technique is used in the sample theme Bluewater, to define the content area.

Build a New Pure PHP Theme

Given the popularity of the PHPTemplate engine, and the extent that it eases the difficulties attendant to theming, it is probably no surprise that few people choose to build their themes without the use of the theme engine. Moreover, pure PHP themes tend to be more difficult to maintain over time and there are fewer help resources available in the Drupal community (as most people employ one of the theme engines). Given the advantages of PHPTemplate, and the drawbacks of building without it, it is very hard to recommend that you build a pure PHP theme; indeed, without some special circumstance, I would recommend against it.

That said, it is possible to build pure PHP templates, without the use of PHPTemplate (or any other theme engine) and in this section we will look at the basics behind this approach to theming, and give you the information you need to get started, should you decide this is how you want to proceed.

If you wish to build a pure PHP theme, there is an example bundled with the default Drupal distro: Chameleon. Neither the Chameleon theme nor its sub-theme Marvin use a theme engine. Note, that while we use Chameleon as a convenient reference, the theme does employ tables and is starting to look a bit old school at this stage. Should you choose to use Chameleon as the starting point of your own PHP theme, you may want to re-visit the formatting.

Building a theme in pure PHP requires a slightly different approach to theming. A number of the functions that would normally be handled by the PHPTemplate engine must be coded into your PHP theme. Open up the file `chameleon.engine` (inside the Chameleon theme) with your editor. When you examine the code, it will be immediately apparent that this is radically different from what we've seen so far in this chapter.

The learning process associated with building PHP themes for Drupal can be challenging unless you have strong PHP skills. For most people, the correct first step will be to crack open the Chameleon directory and copy the elements you need. Copying the code from the Chameleon theme and modifying it to fit your needs is not only a great way to learn but also a huge time saver, as it cuts down dramatically on the chance for errors.

Required Elements

The only required file you need for a pure PHP theme is the `themename.engine` file. This is a plain PHP file and will be placed into the `sites/all/themes/themename` directory. For development purposes, you should also copy into that directory a sample logo; the Drupal logo will work just fine.

The `themename.engine` file begins with the declaration of two functions: `themename_features()` and `themename_regions()`.

The first function is necessary to specify which of the optional theme configuration settings are enabled, the second to enable the Regions. Both of these functions are required.

Let's use the Chameleon theme as our example. The theme configuration options enabled in `chameleon.engine` are: **logo, favicon, name,** and **slogan**. Here's the code that sets that up:

```php
<?php
function chameleon_features() {
    return array(
    'toggle_logo',
```

```
        'toggle_favicon',
        'toggle_name',
        'toggle_slogan');
}
?>
```

This tells the system to enable the **logo, favicon, site name**, and **site slogan** options in the theme configuration settings. You can add others, or delete from this list.

The features available to function `themename_features()` include:

Feature	Functionality
logo	Logo can be used.
toggle_comment_user_picture	Optional display of user picture next to comments.
toggle_logo	Logo can be toggled on or off by administrator.
toggle_mission	Site mission can be toggled on or off by administrator.
toggle_name	Site name can be toggled on or off by administrator.
toggle_node_user_picture	Optional display of user picture next to nodes.
toggle_search	Theme search box can be toggled on or off by administrator.
toggle_slogan	Site slogan can be toggled on or off by administrator.

The second required element is the `themename_regions()` function, which enables the Regions for the theme's Block placement. Turning to the Chameleon theme once again, you will see that the theme only enables two Regions for Block placement: left and right.

```php
<?php
function chameleon_regions() {
    return array(
    'left' => t('left sidebar'),
    'right' => t('right sidebar')
    );
}
?>
```

You can establish whatever Regions you wish to use for the Blocks in your theme by expanding on this, using the same syntax.

Once these functions have been declared, you can begin to place the page elements and the layout.

Note that the Chameleon author also handles a couple of housekeeping matters at the top of the file. First, $title is defined in order to incorporate the Drupal site name and $blocks_left and $blocks_right are provided for use in placing the themed blocks.

HTML Headers

Placing the necessary HTML headers is done with two $output statements, as below:

```
$output   = "<!DOCTYPE html PUBLIC \"-//W3C//DTD XHTML 1.0 Strict//EN\"
\"http://www.w3.org/TR/xhtml1/DTD/xhtml1-strict.dtd\">\n";
$output .= "<html xmlns=\"http://www.w3.org/1999/xhtml\" lang=\
"$language\" xml:lang=\"$language\">\n";
```

Head of Document

The header of the resulting web page needs to incorporate the Drupal head elements, along with the various style sheets and scripts. The code below does this, as well as invoking $title (set earlier in the document), the **site name**, and the **site slogan**.

```
$output .= "<head>\n";
$output .= " <title>". ($title ? strip_tags($title) ." | ". variable_
get("site_name", "Drupal") : variable_get("site_name", "Drupal") ." |
". variable_get("site_slogan", "")) ."</title>\n";
$output .= drupal_get_html_head();
$output .= drupal_get_css();
$output .= drupal_get_js();
$output .= "</head>";
```

Implementing the Features

At the top of the document, the author declared the function chameleon_features(). In addition to declaring the features you must also insert the code to implement the conditions attached to those features and display the resulting output.

Favicon

The author deals with the setting of the Favicon early in the document, prior to the output of the head of the document, and thereby makes the <link rel> tag available to the document head when it is output. All the other features, below, are placed in the body of the page where they will appear in the layout.

```
if (theme_get_setting('toggle_favicon')) {
    drupal_set_html_head('<link rel="shortcut icon" href="'. check_
url(theme_get_setting('favicon')) .'" type="image/x-icon" />');
}
```

Logo

The following conditional statement enables the **logo** to be toggled on or off, wraps the image in an `<a>` tag and also sets the `title` and `alt` attributes.

```
if ($logo = theme_get_setting('logo')) {
    $output .= "  <a href=\"". base_path() ."\" title=\"". t('Home')
."\"><img src=\"$logo\" alt=\"". t('Home') ."\" /></a>";
}
```

Site Name

This snippet enables the **site name** to be toggled on or off, and wraps it with an `H1` tag and a `class`.

```
if (theme_get_setting('toggle_name')) {
    $output .= "  <h1 class=\"site-name title\">". l(variable_
get('site_name', 'drupal'), ""). "</h1>";

}
```

> You have probably noticed by now the recurrence of the `l()` function.
> This function is the key to tying into Drupal's language system and
> enables the system to support multiple languages. Preserve the `l()`
> function in your overrides and code to be able to maintain the system's
> support for multi-lingual labels, error messages, and alerts.

Site Slogan

The following statement enables the **site slogan** to be toggled on or off, and wraps it with a `div` and a `class` for styling.

```
if (theme_get_setting('toggle_slogan')) {

    $output .= "  <div class=\"site-slogan\">". variable_get(
            'site_slogan', '') ."</div>";
}
```

Primary and Secondary Links

Chameleon combines the placement of the primary and secondary links, basically locking the secondary links into a subnavigation role. You don't have to group these two items together in this fashion, but it is one logical option.

Note the snippet below. In both cases, the display of the links is conditional (depending on what is enabled by the administrator). If either one is enabled, then it will appear inside a div with the class navlinks. Additionally, to be able to style each set of links individually, both $primary_links and $secondary_links are provided with a unique class and id.

```
$primary_links = theme('links', menu_primary_links(), array('class' =>
'links', 'id' => 'navlist'));
$secondary_links = theme('links', menu_secondary_links(),
array('class' => 'links', 'id' => 'subnavlist'));
if (isset($primary_links) || isset($secondary_links)) {
    $output .= ' <div class="navlinks">';
    if (isset($primary_links)) {
        $output .= $primary_links;      }
    if (isset($secondary_links)) {
        $output .= $secondary_links;      }
    $output .= " </div>\n";
}
```

Sidebars

The placement of the sidebars is split in the code (reflecting the placement within the table structure) with the left sidebar appearing first, followed by the main content area (discussed below), then the footer (see, below) and finally the right sidebar. The author only declared two Regions for this theme, left and right; as you might expect, those two Regions are placed in the left and right sidebars, respectively.

Sidebar Left

The following places the blocks designated for the left Region into a table cell. Note the conditional statement; this allows the output to be hidden in the event that no blocks are assigned to the Region. For styling, the table cell (td) is given an id named to reflect the placement (sidebar-left).

```
if ($show_blocks && !empty($blocks_left)) {
    $output .= "    <td id=\"sidebar-left\">$blocks_left</td>\n";
}
```

Sidebar Right

This snippet places the blocks designated for the right Region into a table cell. Note the conditional statement; this allows the output to be hidden in the event that no blocks are assigned to the Region. For styling, the table cell (td) is given an id named to reflect the placement (sidebar-right).

```
if ($show_blocks && !empty($blocks_right)) {
    $output .= "    <td id=\"sidebar-right\">$blocks_right</td>\n";
}
```

> Note that the official Drupal site provides an alternative syntax for inserting Regions into your pure PHP theme. See http://www.drupal.org/node/11795.

Main Content Area

The author of Chameleon has set up a number of critical elements to appear inside the main content area. The section will appear as the middle column where there are blocks assigned to both left and right sidebars. The entire set of elements is placed inside a table cell and styled with the id main:

```
$output .= "    <td id=\"main\">\n";
```

Title and Breadcrumb Trail

The author places the **title** and **breadcrumb** together on the page and makes both subject to the appearance of the **title**; the **title** is also wrapped with the <h2> tag.

```
if ($title) {
    $output .= theme("breadcrumb", drupal_get_breadcrumb());
    $output .= "<h2>$title</h2>";
}
```

Tabs

This conditional statement controls the tabs.

```
if ($tabs = theme('menu_local_tasks')) {    $output .= $tabs;
    }
```

Help

This excerpt prints the **help** link:

```
$output .= theme('help');
```

Messages

This excerpt places the output of the **messages** function:

```
$output .= theme('status_messages');
```

Content Region

The content Region is placed below, surrounded by two comment statements:

```
$output .= "\n<!-- begin content -->\n";
$output .= $content;
  $output .= drupal_get_feeds();
$output .= "\n<!-- end content -->\n";
```

Footer

Though the author only declared two Regions, left and right, he includes the footer Region in the code. This provides us with a good example of the function `chameleon_regions()` in action. The function defines which Regions will be available for the administrator to use for the assignment of blocks. In this case, only left and right are options for the administrator, despite the presence of the footer Region in the code. Had the function `chameleon_regions()` been written so as to include `'footer' => t('footer')`, then the Region would be accessible to the administrator for block assignment. As it stands, however, the only output of the code below is the **footer message**, wrapped with a `div`.

```
if ($footer = variable_get('site_footer', '')) {
    $output .= " <div id=\"footer\">$footer</div>\n";
}
```

Theme Closure

You must close the page properly, adding the `theme_closure()` function and the closing `<body>` and `<html>` tags. The final line renders the page.

```
$output .=  theme_closure();
$output .= " </body>\n";
$output .= "</html>\n";
return $output;
```

Overriding Functions

You can override Drupal's default theme functions in your pure PHP theme. The process of creating overrides is almost identical to that used in a PHPTemplate theme: copy the function, rename it, and make your changes. The only difference is where you place the overrides. In a pure PHP theme you place the overrides in the `themename.engine` file.

Turning to `chameleon.engine` again for an example, we find that the theme provides overrides for the `node`, `comment`, and `help` functions.

Themeable function	Name of override
theme_comment	chameleon_comment
theme_help	chameleon_help
theme_node	chameleon_node

In each case, the original function has been copied from its source, then pasted into the `chameleon.engine` file, renamed, and modified as desired.

Summary

This chapter has taken us from a blank page to a completely functional theme. We've covered how to build a PHPTemplate-powered theme from scratch, and illustrated how to further extend this (or any other PHPTemplate) theme. The role of variables in themes was discussed as was dynamic theming and styling. This chapter also touched on building themes without the use of a theme engine.

8
Dealing with Forms

In this chapter, we look at the forms generated by the Drupal core and how they can be themed. This chapter covers all the default forms available on the front end of the website, including the various search, login, and contact forms, as well as the output of the Polls module. It's worth noting at the outset that this chapter is about theming forms, not creating custom forms; accordingly, the contents of this chapter are concerned with presentation not with adding or deleting form elements or creating new forms.

There are no additional files to download or install for this chapter; all examples are based on the default Garland theme. You will, however, need, access to your favorite editor to make the modifications discussed here, as well as a Drupal installation on which to preview your work.

How Forms Work in Drupal

With Drupal 5, the approach to form handling continues to evolve. Drupal forms are tightly integrated into the core, and as a result, theming them can be a bit of a chore. Unlike other areas of the system, most forms are not the subject of a variety of pre-existing themeable functions. Instead, if you wish to theme a form you are typically left with the choice of either working directly with the form functions in the Drupal core or with following the well-trodden path of intercepting and overriding the form output using the power of the PHPTemplate template engine.

While themeable functions are pretty easy to deal with—being essentially concerned with the formatting of output—the Drupal form functions tend to be rather complicated. Finding the proper bit to modify and then accomplishing that without unintended side effects requires either a solid knowledge of PHP or a willingness to experiment, combined with a great deal of patience.

While you will note that a number of functions are mentioned in this chapter, most of them specific to a particular form, the global function `drupal_render` is worthy of particular mention. This function produces form output throughout the system and is one of the keys to theming your forms.

At first glance, the function doesn't volunteer much information. Look at this example of the function in action, in this case providing the output of the user login block:

```
function phptemplate_user_login_block($form) {
    $output = drupal_render($form);
return $output;
}
```

In this example, we have created an override to the form function. This override would be placed inside the `template.php` file. As written, the override does nothing other than produce the output of the form. The important points to note here are:

1. You can place the form output with this simple statement and then add HTML around it easily.

2. As you can see above, there are no visible options for controlling individual form elements in this basic formulation; to style individual form elements you must do more.

3. If you are using PHPTemplate, you also have the option to set up a dedicated template (`.tpl.php`) to hold this function and any modifications.

To achieve a greater degree of control over the styling, we need to go behind the scenes a bit, to look at what goes on when the system invokes this function.

 drupal_render supersedes the old function `form_render`, which was used in earlier Drupal systems.

For the sake of discussion, let's take a look at an example of an unaltered Drupal form function and examine it in more detail.

Here's the function that produces the user Login Form that appears in a Block. The form ID for this form is `user_login_block` and the original code can be found in `modules/user/user.module`:

```
function user_login_block() {
    $form = array(
        '#action' => url($_GET['q'], drupal_get_destination()),
        '#id' => 'user-login-form',
        '#base' => 'user_login',
    );
```

```
$form['name'] = array('#type' => 'textfield',
    '#title' => t('Username'),
    '#maxlength' => USERNAME_MAX_LENGTH,
    '#size' => 15,
    '#required' => TRUE,
);
$form['pass'] = array('#type' => 'password',
    '#title' => t('Password'),
    '#maxlength' => 60,
    '#size' => 15,
    '#required' => TRUE,
);
$form['submit'] = array('#type' => 'submit',
    '#value' => t('Log in'),
);
$items = array();
if (variable_get('user_register', 1)) {
    $items[] = l(t('Create new account'), 'user/register',
                array('title' => t('Create a new user account.')));
}
$items[] = l(t('Request new password'), 'user/password',
            array('title' => t('Request new password via e-mail.')));
$form['links'] = array('#value' => theme('item_list', $items));
return $form;
}
```

Note how this function sets the attributes for the various fields, including field lengths and data labels. The snippet below, for example, produces the password field and its related attributes:

```
$form['pass'] = array('#type' => 'password',
    '#title' => t('Password'),
    '#maxlength' => 60,
    '#size' => 15,
    '#required' => TRUE,
);
```

Here is the code for the production of the submit button:

```
$form['submit'] = array('#type' => 'submit',
    '#value' => t('Log in'),
);
```

This snippet sets the text for the links at the bottom of the form:

```
$items[] = l(t('Request new password'), 'user/password',
array('title' => t('Request new password via e-mail.')));
```

All of these items can be modified by intercepting and overriding this function, as discussed below. The trick is locating the form ID of the original item you wish to change and then identifying the elements (e.g., the password field or the submit button, etc.) that you wish to override.

> If you really want to get into the nuts and bolts of Drupal forms, check out the forms section of the Drupal API: `http://api.drupal.org/?q=api/file/developer/topics/forms_api.html/5`.

Modifying and Overriding Form Functions

The key to obtaining flexibility in the theming of Drupal forms lies in the creation and manipulation of theme functions specific to a particular form. As already noted, the forms have few pre-existing themeable functions. There are some exceptions, for example the generic functions found in `forms.inc`, and the dedicated functions for the Search Forms and the Polls module, but by and large the theming of forms must be accomplished without the benefit of dedicated themeable functions.

To get control over what is happening inside the form — the fields, the data labels, etc. — you have to create your own overrides to modify specific elements of the form function in question.

> For basic changes to the styling of a form, you may not need to create a new function; you may be able to achieve your goals through manipulation of the default styling in the CSS, as discussed below.

It is possible to create overrides and make modifications to the various form functions. To do this, you must first identify the relevant function, then find exactly what it is you want to modify, then create the override.

Once you have identified what you want to change, you are faced with a choice as to how best to accomplish the modifications. Broadly speaking, your options are:

1. Adding HTML via Function Attributes
2. Using `form_alter()` and creating a new module to hold your new form function
3. Overriding the function from within `template.php`
4. Creating a new template (`.tpl.php` file) to control your form presentation

Each option has pros and cons and each is discussed in the pages that follow.

Adding HTML via Function Attributes

The Drupal form API makes provisions for you to be able to add basic HTML to a form via a limited set of attributes named #prefix, #suffix, and #markup. These attributes are invoked from inside the function; accordingly, this approach to modifying forms is used most frequently by developers when they create the form.

- #prefix is used to add HTML before a form element.

- #suffix is used to add HTML after an element.

- #markup allows you to declare HTML as type #markup in the form.

This approach is generally less preferred, as it less flexible and harder to maintain going forward. If you are looking to modify an existing form, the better practice is to create a function, as per the discussions below.

Using form_alter()

The function form_alter() allows you to add to, subtract from, and modify the contents of a form. This is a powerful tool and is not dependent upon the use of PHPTemplate. At its most basic, form_alter is very useful for modifying the data labels and text that appear with the form. Additionally, if you wish to extensively modify a form, this function gives you an easy avenue for creating custom fields.

form_alter opens up some interesting possibilities, though the use of the function varies from how we have approached theming problems elsewhere in this book. To use the function, you will need to create a new module.

Creating a new module to hold your form modifications may initially sound like a lot of extra work, but it's not as bad as it sounds. While a detailed discussion of building modules is beyond the scope of this book, let's take a run at illustrating this handy technique with a simple example.

Assume we wish to do the following:

1. Change the data labels on our Login Form
2. Change the wording on the submit button of the Login Form
3. Change the wording on the submit button of the User Registration Form
4. Change the wording of the data label for the Request Password Form

To accomplish these basic changes, we can either isolate and modify the user_login function, the user_register function, and the user_pass function, or we can create one new module, implement form_alter(), and make all our required changes in one place.

> If you wish to modify only one form, it may be easier to directly override the form; however, if you want to modify more than one form, form_alter() is the way to go as it allows you to place all the modifications in one file.

To create our new module and implement form_alter(), we have to do the following:

First, create a new directory to hold the custom module. If it does not already exist, create a directory named modules and place it inside sites/all. Now create a directory with your module name and place it inside sites/all/modules. Let's name this new module formmod.

Next, we need to create a .info file for the benefit of Drupal—the system needs some basic information about our module. Name the file formmod.info and save it to our formmod directory. The contents of the file should be as follows:

```
; $Id$
name = FormMod
description = Contains modifications to the site forms.
package = Packt
version = "$Name$"
```

Note in the code above that I have specified our new module's name for the name field. I have added a description as well, which will appear in the administration interface (in the Module Manager). The value for package is used to determine where this module will appear in the groupings of modules inside the Module Manager. In this case, I have created a new group named Packt. The version field value should always be as it appears in our example.

Next, let's create a new file and name it formmod.module—this is where we will add the function and our modifications. Here are the contents of the file:

```
<?php
//$Id$
/**
 * @file
 * Adds modifications to various site forms.
 *
 */
function formmod_form_alter($form_id, &$form) {
    // This part changes the user login form
    if ($form_id == 'user_login') {
        // Change the text below the username field to 'Enter your
        // username.'
        $form['name']['#description'] = 'Enter your username.';
        // Change the text on the submit button to 'enter'
```

```
        $form['submit']['#value'] = 'enter';
    }
    // This part changes the user registration form
    if ($form_id == 'user_register') {
        // Change the text on the submit button to 'submit registration'
        $form['submit']['#value'] = 'submit registration';
    }
    // This part changes the request password form
    if ($form_id == 'user_pass') {
        // Changes the data label to add basic instructions to form
        $form['name']['#title'] =
            'Enter your username or email address, then click submit.';
        // Change the text on the submit button to 'request password'
        $form['submit']['#value'] = 'request password';
    }
}
```

After you have entered the contents, save the file to the `formmod` directory.

 Note that this module file opens with a php tag, but *does not* include a closing tag; this is intentional and necessary to avoid formatting problems.

The last step is to log in to the admin system and head over to the Module manager (**Administer | Site building | Modules**). Scroll down the list of modules and you will find a new section named **Packt**, along with our new module, **FormMod**. You must activate the module and click save to enable this module. Once you have completed this step, the changes made to the forms will be immediately visible.

Overriding Form Functions from template.php

 For a list of themeable functions applicable to forms, see Chapter 4.

You can create your own functions for forms, thereby overriding the original function and giving you the opportunity to apply modified styling or add additional HTML. Basic function overrides can either be placed in the `template.php` file, or made the subject of dedicated template files. In this section, we will discuss the former technique; in the next section, the latter.

As in so many other areas of the Drupal system, the naming convention is the key to the system recognizing the presence of your function override. Use the following naming convention for your new function:

```
function theme_form_id($form)
```

As an example: The form ID of the Login Block Form is `user_login_block`. Accordingly, if you wish to override the function that controls the form (and you are using PHPTemplate!) you would name your function as follows:

```
function phptemplate_user_login_block($form)
```

The function would be placed in the theme's `template.php` file.

Let's now work through the mechanics of a basic example and override the output function for the user login block.

Open your `template.php` file and add the following:

```
function phptemplate_user_login_block($form) {
    $output = drupal_render($form);
return $output;
}
```

Save the file and you're done. This code now controls the output of the user login block. As written above, the new function adds nothing to the form output and will show only the default output. You can now add to that function as you see fit, adding additional classes or text that will be rendered with the form. For example, let's add a `div` to give us a few more options for styling this form:

```
function phptemplate_user_login_block($form) {
    return '<div id="login-block-form">'. drupal_render($form) .'</
div>';
}
```

The example above is basic, and modifies only the form as a whole. What if you want to change the form elements?

To make changes to the form elements, you will need to go one further step. As an example, let's modify the data labels associated with our Login Block form. Add the following to the function we put in the `template.php` file:

```
function phptemplate_user_login_block($form) {
    $items = array();
        if (variable_get('user_register', 1)) {
        $items[] = l(t('Create new account'), 'user/register',
                array('title' => t('Create a new user account.')));
        }
    $items[] = l(t('Send password reminder'), 'user/password',
            array('title' => t('Request new password via e-mail.')));
    $form['links'] = array('#value' => theme('item_list', $items));
        return _phptemplate_callback('user-login-block',
            array('form' => $form));
}
```

This code does several things. First, it checks to see whether this user is logged in. Second, it modifies the text associated with the user register and password reminder links. Finally, it creates a callback to a specific dedicated template for the form, `user-login-block.tpl.php`

 Note in the preceding example, if you did not wish to redirect to a template file, you could simply substitute `return drupal_render($form);` for the last line in the example.

The approach just outlined is not necessarily intuitive, and may be difficult for non-programmers to maintain. As a general rule, if the modifications tend to be complex, or there is a need to be able to maintain the form easily, then you are better off creating a dedicated template, as discussed in the next section.

Creating Custom Templates for Forms

With the help of PHPTemplate, we can create custom templates for either the pages, or the Blocks in which the forms are displayed, or even the forms themselves.

Page Templates

Many of the forms in the default Drupal system appear inside the content area of pages. For those forms, it is sometimes desirable to provide dedicated page templates. In most cases this is a straightforward matter; we treat it like any other page template override.

 Overriding page templates is discussed in depth in Chapters 7.

By way of example, let's set up a dedicated page template for the site-wide contact form.

First, create the page template where your form will appear. It's easiest just to copy the existing `page.tpl.php`, rename it `page-contact.tpl.php`, and save it to the root directory of your theme. Make your changes to the new template file and you are done. The system will automatically give precedence to the more specific `page-contact.tpl.php` and display it instead of the default `page.tpl.php`.

While the contact form is a simple job, the combined nature of the Login Page form, Request Password Form, and User Registration Form presents some special challenges for providing a dedicated page template. It can be done, but you need to include some logic to enable the template to work logically.

The function `_phptemplate_variables()` comes in handy in this situation. We can implement the page hook to add additional logic that helps determine whether the user is already logged in.

Add the following to your `template.php` file:

```
function _phptemplate_variables($hook, $variables = array()) {
  switch ($hook) {
    case 'page':
      global $user;
      if (arg(0) == 'user'){
        if (!$user->uid) { //only shows the page to users who are not
                           // logged in
          $variables['template_file'] = 'page-login';
        }
        elseif (arg(1) == 'login' || arg(1) == 'register' ||
                arg(1) == 'password' ) {
          $variables['template_file'] = 'page-login';
        }
      }
      break;
  }

  return $variables;
}
```

Next, create a copy of your `page.tpl.php` file and save it as a new template file named `page-login.tpl.php`. Make your changes to the new page template and save the file.

 Note that you could also override the default `page.tpl.php` with the file `page-user.tpl.php`. The system would automatically apply the new template for all output generated by the user module—including the Login Page Form. This is not the result we want, however, as the user module includes not only the Login, Register, and Request Password pages, but also various other user-related pages. In the above example, we have avoided the unwanted styling of other unrelated pages by targeting the Login page.

Block Templates

Just as you can create a custom template for a page, you can also create a custom template for a block. As we discussed in Chapter 7, overriding a block template is a relatively simple matter. We need to create the template (`.tpl.php`), name it properly, then let Drupal do the rest.

Overriding block templates is discussed in depth in Chapter 7.

The Polls module, the Search Block Form, and the Login Block Form are all forms that are displayed as blocks. It is conceivable that you may want to provide a dedicated Block template for any of them.

By way of example, let's assume you want to provide a customized template for the Search Block.

First, create your new template file. Name it `block-search.tpl.php`. For the contents of the file, let's copy and paste the contents of the theme's original `block. tpl.php` file and insert a custom style (highlighted below):

```
<div id="block-<?php print $block->module .'-'. $block->delta; ?>"
class="clear-block block block-<?php print $block->module ?>">
<?php if ($block->subject): ?>
   <h2><?php print $block->subject ?></h2>
<?php endif;?>
   <div class="search-block"><?php print $block->content ?></div>
</div>
```

Save this file to your theme directory and you are done; the presentation of the Search Block is now controlled by your new Block template.

Templates for Forms Output

While PHPTemplate allows us to set up page and block templates with very little coding, we can go a step further and with a bit of additional work, establish templates for the forms themselves, thereby allowing us the freedom to modify the form output with greater granularity.

As an example, let's modify the Search Block Form. To do this, we will need to use the `phptemplate_callback` to call our custom template file.

First, let's set up the callback. Add the following to your `template.php` file:

```
function phptemplate_search_block_form($form) {
   return _phptemplate_callback('search-block-form', array('form' =>
$form));
}
```

This code works by associating the form ID (`search_block_form`) with a specific template (`search-block-form`).

Next, create a new template file. Name the new template `search-block-form.tpl.php` (consistent with what we called it in the function we added to `template.php`, earlier). Save the file to your theme directory.

With this new template, we can do a number of things, for example, adding some text, altering the input box, and changing the text on the submit button:

```
<h3>Search this site</h3>
<input type="text" maxlength="128" name="search_block_form_keys"
id="edit-search_block_form_keys"  size="25" value="" title="Enter the
terms then click Go!" class="form-text" />
<input type="submit" name="op" value="Go!"  />
```

How did we know what to place in this file to alter the form fields? The answer is simple: View the source code via the view source command in your browser, then copy the lines you want to change and paste them into the new template, where you can modify them as needed!

Common Form Issues

In this section, we look at areas of common concern with forms, that is, how to change the text information associated with the default forms, how to alter the styling of forms, and how to use images for form buttons. In the process, we compare and contrast the different approaches introduced earlier and note some special issues.

Modifying Data Labels and Other Text

One of the most commonly requested form modifications is the ability to change the data labels and explanatory text built into the default forms. There are several alternative ways to modify the text elements. The choice of which technique to apply depends largely on the number of changes you wish to make and degree to which you will need to be able to administer the text through the admin interface.

Using form_alter()

As we saw earlier in this chapter, you can create a custom module and use `form_alter` to make changes to one or more forms. This approach is very useful where you want to make changes across several forms or if you wish to combine text changes with more extreme form modifications (e.g., adding or deleting fields). However, if your goal is simply to insert new text not related to a specific field, or if you wish to modify only one form, you are probably better served by one of the other approaches outlined next.

Override the Function

If you have only limited changes to make to one form, creating a specific override to the form function in your `template.php` file may be your preferred solution. Basic modifications can be managed easily from within `template.php`, without the need to create a custom module or a dedicated template.

Create a New Template

If you wish to add new text or HTML around your form, the creation of a new template is likely to be your best solution. A separate dedicated `.tpl.php` file is easy to theme as you need.

Add a Node

Adding text to a form can be done easily by modifying the form itself, as seen. However, placing the text inside a module or a page template file makes it difficult for non-programmers to edit. To gain maximum flexibility, the better approach is to create an editable node for your content, then have the system display that with the form. The process is simple and, considering how significantly it eases site management, is highly recommended. Here's how it works.

For the purposes of this example, assume you wish to add a Terms of Use clause to your User Registration Form.

First, create a new node to contain the content. Title the node **Terms of Use** and then add some appropriate legalese, for example:

The opinions expressed by users herein are exclusively their own.

After you save your text, note the node number. In the development server setup that I am using, the number of this new node is 2.

Next, open `template.php` and enter the following, in order to make the node available to the template file:

```
function phptemplate_user_register($form) {
    $login_node = node_load(array( 'nid' => 2));
        return _phptemplate_callback('user-register', array(
                'form' => $form,
                'login_node' => $login_node
    ));
}
```

Finally, let's print the new variable in the form. Create a new template to override the default User Registration Form output. Name your new file `user-register.tpl.php` and save it to your theme directory. The contents of the file are as follows:

```
<h1><?php print $login_node->title; ?></h1>
<?php
    print $login_node->body;
?>
<?php
    print_r(drupal_render($form));
?>
```

Your new User Registration Form will look something like this:

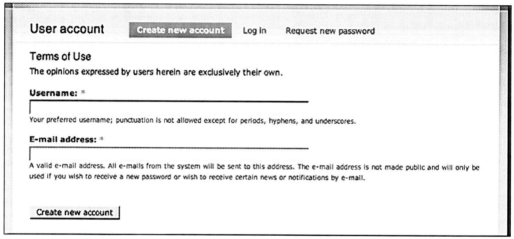

Note the appearance of our node content immediately above the form fields.

The site administrator can now modify the text easily through the content management interface, without the need for further coding. To apply this technique to other forms, simply create the appropriate `.tpl.php` file (to override the original output) and modify the code added to `template.php` to name the new override.

Modifying the Styling of a Form

All of the forms, excepting the contact forms, have dedicated style sheets. The primary selectors affecting each form are defined in their respective style sheets.

Form	Primary style sheet
contact us	`modules/system/system.css`
login	`modules/user/user.css`
request password	`modules/user/user.css`

Form	Primary style sheet
polls	`modules/poll/poll.css`
search	`modules/search/search.css`
user edit	`modules/user/user.css`
user registration	`modules/user/user.css`

Overriding the CSS styling for forms is no different than overriding the CSS for other areas of your Drupal site. Simply identify the elements that need to be modified and place your new definitions in your theme's `style.css` file.

Using form_alter()

You can use `form_alter()` to inject custom style definitions inside your form, but this approach is probably not the best way to deal with this issue. Apart from special needs, your best approach is to either create a function override from within `template.php` and include your changes or to create a new template.

Override the Function

Placing the override inside `template.php` and allowing the function to render the form without the necessity of a callback to a dedicated template file is the most direct method of making the change, though it may not be the simplest path.

Create a New Template

If you wish to provide unique selectors that allow you to style the form distinctly, creating a new `.tpl.php` file is a good approach that is easy to execute and easy to maintain.

Using Images for Buttons

If you want to use images for the submit button of a form, you must make two changes to your `template.php` file (and of course you need to provide an image).

The first bit of code is necessary to overcome several issues in the system and to provide proper IDs for the image. The code creates a new generic theme function that enables the use of images for the submit buttons throughout your site:

```
function phptemplate_button($element) {
// following lines are copied directly from form.inc core file:
// Make sure not to overwrite classes
if (isset($element['#attributes']['class'])) {
```

```
    $element['#attributes']['class'] = 'form-'.
       $element['#button_type'] .' '. $element['#attributes']['class'];
}
else {
    $element['#attributes']['class'] =
            'form-'. $element['#button_type'];
}
// My change is type="' . (($element['#button_type'] == "image") ?
// 'image' : 'submit' ) . '"
   return '<input type="' . (($element['#button_type'] == "image")
? 'image' : 'submit' ) . '" '. (empty($element['#name']) ? '' :
'name="'. $element['#name'] .'" ')  .'id="'. $element['#id'].'"
value="'. check_plain($element['#value']) .'" '. drupal_attributes($el
ement['#attributes']) ." />\n";
}
```

The code for the function `phptemplate_button` was originally published on the Drupal.org site and is included in the snippets section. This is worth watching for additional discussion and revisions from the community. Visit http://drupal.org/node/144758.

Now, by way of example, let's set up the use of an image for the submit button of our theme Search Form. Add the following to your `template.php` file:

```
function phptemplate_search_theme_form($form) {
    $form['submit']['#theme'] = 'button';
    $form['submit']['#button_type'] = 'image';
    $form['submit']['#attributes'] = array(
        'src' => base_path() . path_to_theme() . '/images/btn-search-
          submit.png', //the name and location of your button image
        'alt' => t('Search')  //the alt text for the image
    );
    return drupal_render($form);
}
```

Now, assuming you have an image uploaded to the proper directory, you should be done. Note that you will need to repeat this exercise for each form where you wish to use an image for the submit button.

The Default Forms

The default Drupal distro includes a number of forms for the front-end user. Some are active at installation, others need to be enabled and configured by the administrator. On the following pages, we go through the default forms and provide a quick look at each, giving the information you need to work on and highlighting any special concerns unique to each particular form.

The User Forms

The user forms consist of the Login Forms, the User Registration Form, the Request Password Form, and the User Information Editing Form. All the functions relating to the user forms are found at `modules/user/user.module`.

The Login Forms

The Login Form exists in two varieties: The Login Block Form and the Login Page Form.

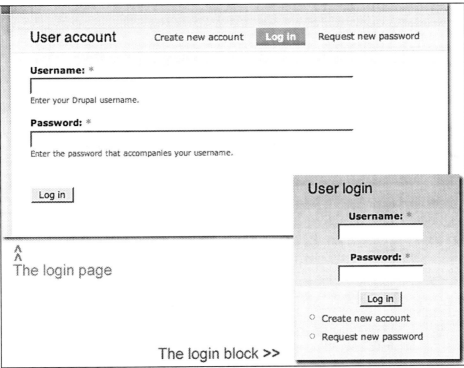

The Login Form appears both as a Block (aka, the Login Block Form) and in the content region (aka, the Login Page Form). Note the Login Page also includes links to new account registration (aka, the User Registration Form) and the Request Password Form.

The Login Block Form

The function that builds this form is `user_login_block`, which is located at `modules/user/user.module`.

The styling of the Login Block Form is predominantly managed by the selectors defined in the file `modules/user/user.css`. See Appendix A for a listing of the contents of that file.

The Login Page Form

In addition to the block position, the Login Form can also occupy a page position. In the page position, the Login Form is controlled by the function `user_login`, located at `modules/user/user.module`.

The styling of the Login Page form is predominantly managed by the selectors defined in the file `modules/user/user.css`. See Appendix A for a listing of the contents of that file.

The User Registration Form

The User Registration Form appears in the content region and can be reached from either the link in the Login block or from the links at the top of the Login Form and the Request Password Form.

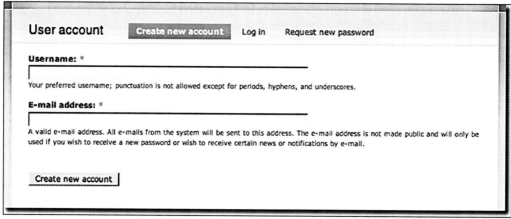

The user registration form appears in page mode only.

This form is generated by the function `user_register`, found at `modules/user.module`.

The styling of the User Registration Form is predominantly managed by the selectors defined in the file `modules/user/user.css`. See Appendix A for a listing of the contents of that file.

The Request Password Form

The Request Password Form appears in the content region and can be reached from either the link in the Login Block or from the links at the top of the Login Form and the User Registration Form.

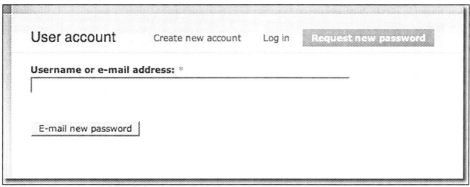

The Request Password Form appears in the content region.

The function that controls the output of the Request Password Form is `user_pass` at `modules/user.module`.

The styling of the Request Password Form is predominantly managed by the selectors defined in the file `modules/user/user.css`. See Appendix A for a listing of the contents of that file.

The Edit User Info Form

Registered users of a Drupal site are able to maintain their personal information themselves via the account information screen.

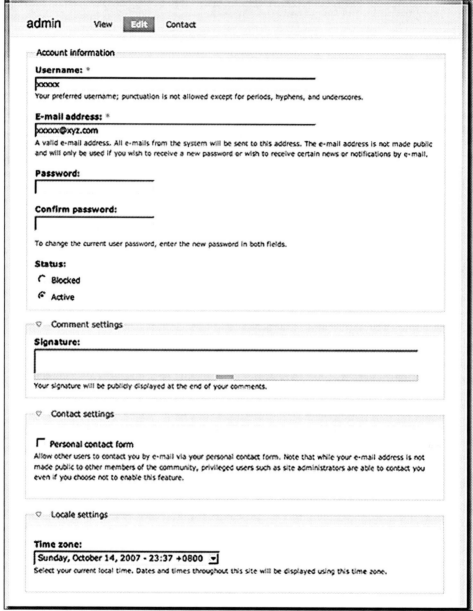

The Edit User Info Form is accessible by registered users and appears in the content region. The particular form shown here is for the admin user and includes the option to toggle the status of the user between active and blocked. Users with lower privileges will not see this option.

The function that controls the output of the Edit User Info Form is `user_edit_form` found at `modules/user.module`.

The styling of the edit User Info Form is predominantly managed by the selectors defined in the file `modules/user/user.css`. See Appendix A for a listing of the contents of that file.

The Default Contact Form

Drupal includes a Contact module that can be used to generate one or more contact forms for your site.

The default Drupal Contact Form.

The function that controls the output of the Contact Form is `contact_site_page` found at `modules/contact/contact.module`.

The styling of the Contact Form is predominantly managed by the selectors defined in the file `modules/system/system.css`. See Appendix A for a listing of the contents of that file.

The Search Forms

The Search Forms have several unique characteristics that set them apart from the other forms in Drupal. The first unique characteristic is their number and variety: There are multiple variations of the Search Form in the system. The second is the fact that the Search Forms are the subject of several themeable functions, and finally, the Search Forms also have an output that we have to consider, that is, the Search Results page.

There are four versions of the Search Form in the default Drupal distro:

1. The Theme Search Form is generally placed near the top of the page (a decision made by the theme developer) and subsequently enabled/disabled by the configuration settings.

2. The Block Search Form is produced by the search module and is typically placed in a sidebar region. (Before the search block will appear on the site, the corresponding module must be enabled by the administrator and the search block assigned to an active region.)

3. The Page Search Form appears in the content region of a page. While the search page is just a basic one-line search box, the search page also has a link to the advanced search functionality, which is a more complex variation on the basic Search Form.

4. The Advanced Search Form always appears in the content area in search page format (assuming the user has been granted access to the advanced search functionality by the administrator).

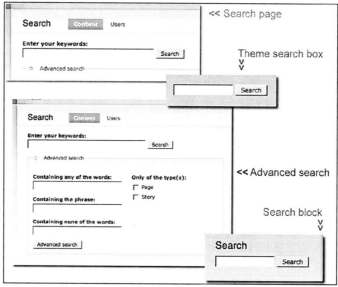

The various Search Forms as they appear in the default Garland theme.

The majority of the functions relating to the Search Forms are found in `modules/search/search.module`. The Search Forms also have available several themeable functions. Unfortunately, the themeable search functions are rather limited, consisting of just a simple `div` wrapping the form output. While the themeable functions are useful in that they provide some assistance with CSS, they give you no granular control over the output formatting of the form elements.

Item	Themeable function
search block form	`theme_search_block_form`
page search form	`theme_search_page`
search results	`theme_search_item`
theme search box	`theme_search_theme_form`

The Theme Search Form

The Theme Search Form typically appears somewhere near the top of the theme — where it has been placed by the theme developer.

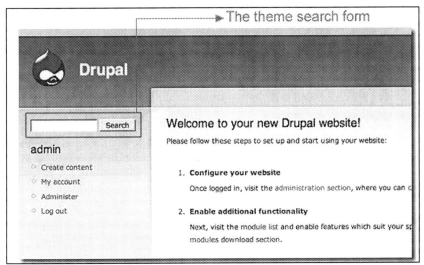

In Garland the Theme Search Form appears at the top of the left column, making it easily mistaken for the search block (as though the search block was assigned to the left sidebar region).

The form is produced by the function `search_theme_form`, located at `modules/search/search.module`.

The function `theme_search_theme_form` wraps the Theme Search Form with the following:

```
<div class="container-inline"></div>
```

The styling of the Search Forms is predominantly managed by the selectors defined in the file `modules/search/search.css`. See Appendix A for a listing of the contents of that file.

The Block Search Form

The Block Search Form is often visually similar to the Theme Search Form, but the key point to note here is that this is controlled by the search module and must be assigned to a block position. Like other blocks, a title can also be specified by the administrator via the Block manager.

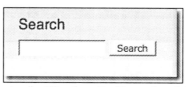

The Block Search Form often visually differs from the Theme Search Form in only one regard: the presence of the block title (in the default Garland implementation, above, "Search").

The Block Search Form is produced by the function `search_block_form`, located at `modules/search/search.module`.

The function `theme_search_block_form` wraps the Block Search Form with the following:

```
<div class="container-inline"></div>
```

The styling of the Search Forms is predominantly managed by the selectors defined in the file `modules/search/search.css`. See Appendix A for a listing of the contents of that file.

The Page Search Form

The Page Search Form provides a basic search box, but with the addition of an advanced search link and the option to search for other content or users.

The Page Search Form always appears in the content region.

The Page Search Form is produced by the function `search_form`, located at `modules/search/search.module`.

The styling of the Search Forms is predominantly managed by the selectors defined in the file `modules/search/search.css`. See Appendix A for a listing of the contents of that file.

The Advanced Search Form

Clicking on the advanced search link on the Page Search Form brings the user to the Advanced Search Form, which includes a number of new options for searching the site.

More options appear here—and more formatting issues. The Advanced Search Form appears in the content region.

The Advanced Search Form is produced by the function `search_form`, working in conjunction with the code in the `node.module` file, located at `modules/node/node.module` (to find the specific elements unique to the advanced Search Form, look in the node module).

The styling of the Search Forms is predominantly managed by the selectors defined in the file `modules/search/search.css`. See Appendix A for a listing of the contents of that file.

The Search Results Page

The search results page is produced by the various Search Forms. The functions that control the output are contained in `modules/search/search.module`. The function `search_view` collects the results and provides the page titles and related info. The functions `theme_search_page` and `theme_search_item` are also provided to make it easier to style the search results.

The styling of the search results is predominantly managed by the selectors defined in the file `modules/search/search.css`. See Appendix A for a listing of the contents of that file.

The Poll Module Forms

The Poll module involves several forms. The two we will deal with here are the Poll Block Form and the Poll Page Form.

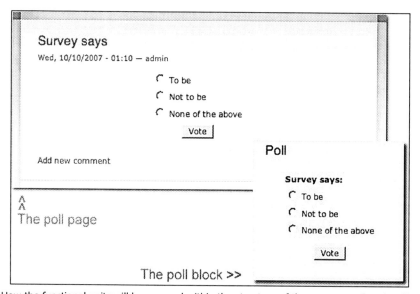

How the functional units will be grouped within the structure of the `page.tpl.php` file.

Drupal provides several themeable functions that affect the Poll module. Unlike the bare-bones themeable functions provided for the Search Forms, the functions for the Poll module give you a great deal of control. Among the functions to note here, all located in `modules/poll/poll.module`, are:

- `theme_poll_bar`
- `theme_poll_view_voting`
- `theme_poll_view_results`

The Poll Block Form

The Poll Block Form appears when the administrator has enabled both the Poll module and assigned the Poll Block to an active region.

The Poll Block Form is produced by the function `poll_block`, which is located at `modules/poll/poll.module`, but note as well the themeable functions mentioned at the beginning of the section on polls.

The styling of the Poll Block Form is predominantly managed by the selectors defined in the file `modules/poll/poll.css`. See Appendix A for a listing of the contents of that file.

The Poll Page Form

The Poll Page Form appears whenever a visitor clicks on the poll or if the administrator has provided a menu item linking to a page containing the poll content item.

The Poll Page Form is produced by the function `poll_form`, which is located at `modules/poll/poll.module`, but note as well the themeable functions mentioned at the beginning of the section on polls.

The styling of the Poll Page Form is predominantly managed by the selectors defined in the file `modules/poll/poll.css`. See Appendix A for a listing of the contents of that file.

Summary

This chapter has covered one of the more challenging areas of Drupal theming, that is, theming the forms. The default Drupal forms covered in this chapter can be styled through the application of a variety of techniques, both with and without the assistance of PHPTemplate.

In this chapter, we looked at the various theming techniques and identified the key components associated with each task and where to find them. We also introduced the idea of creating a module to control form modifications, via the function `form_alter`.

Appendix A

The following is a listing of all the selectors in the various style sheets. This list reflects the default distro and is current for Drupal 5.2.

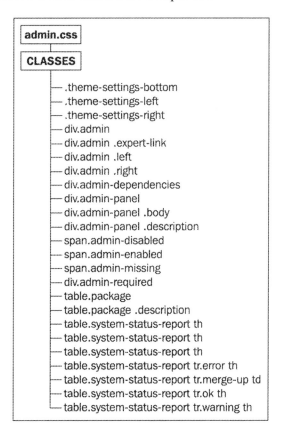

```
admin.css

CLASSES

    .theme-settings-bottom
    .theme-settings-left
    .theme-settings-right
    div.admin
    div.admin .expert-link
    div.admin .left
    div.admin .right
    div.admin-dependencies
    div.admin-panel
    div.admin-panel .body
    div.admin-panel .description
    span.admin-disabled
    span.admin-enabled
    span.admin-missing
    div.admin-required
    table.package
    table.package .description
    table.system-status-report th
    table.system-status-report th
    table.system-status-report th
    table.system-status-report tr.error th
    table.system-status-report tr.merge-up td
    table.system-status-report tr.ok th
    table.system-status-report tr.warning th
```

`/modules/system/admin.css`

Concerns primarily the elements unique to the administration interface.

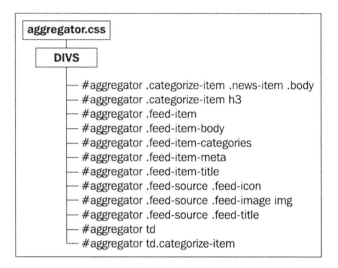

`/modules/aggregator/aggregator.css`

Relates to the Aggregator Module.

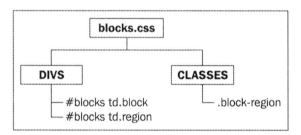

`/modules/block/block.css`

Relates to the formatting of Blocks.

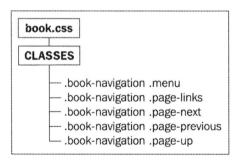

`/modules/book/book.css`

Concerns Book node content.

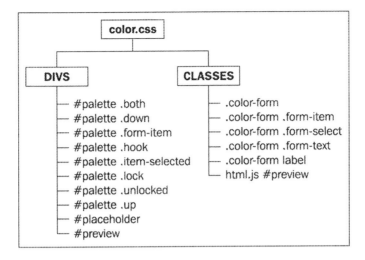

`/modules/color/color.css`

Relates to the Color Module.

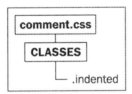

`/modules/comment/comment.css`

A single selector relevant to Comments.

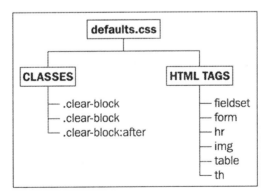

`/modules/system/default.css`

Provides basic HTML style definitions common to many areas in the system.

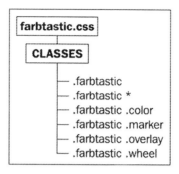

`/misc/farbtastic/farbtastic.css`

Relates to the Farbtastic color picker.

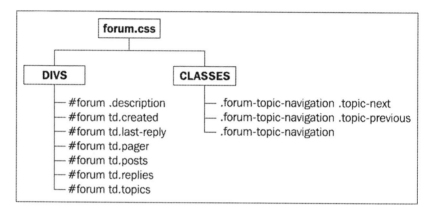

`/modules/forum/forum.css`

Concerns the Forum Module.

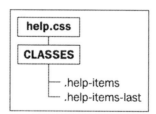

`/modules/help/help.css`

Classes for Help items.

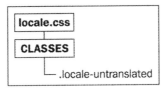

`/modules/locale/locale.css`

One selector for the Locale Module.

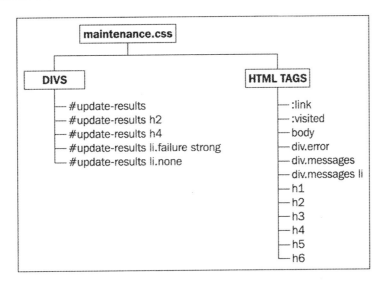

`/misc/maintenance.css`

Relates to the Maintenance page.

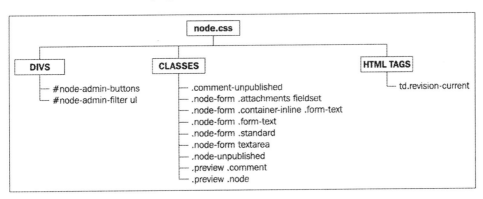

`/modules/node/node.css`

Provides selectors for the Nodes.

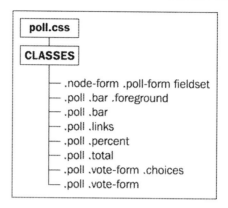

`/modules/poll/poll.css`

Concerns the Polls Module.

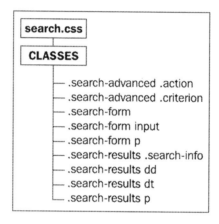

`/modules/search/search.css`

Styling for the various Search functions.

/modules/system/system.css

A collection of common styles.

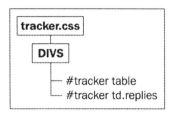

`/modules/tracker/tracker.css`

Selectors for the Tracker Module.

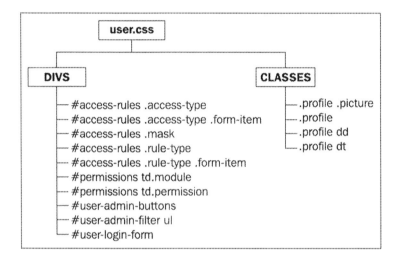

`/modules/user/user.css`

Relates to the User and Profile Modules.

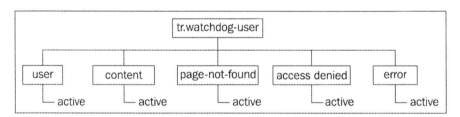

`/modules/watchdog/watchdog.css`

Concerns the Watchdog Module.

Index

A

additional theme
finding 25-27
installing 28-32
Aggregator Module functions
theme_aggregator_block_item 87
theme_aggregator_feed 87
theme_aggregator_page_item 87
theme_aggregator_page_list 87
theme_aggregator_summary_item 87
approaches, overrides
files, intercepting 111
files, substituting 111
overrides, placing in dedicated files 113-115
overrides, placing in theme template.php file 112
PHPTemplate engine files, modifying 113

B

Block Module functions
theme_block_admin_display 88
blocks
managing 38
PHP, adding 45, 46
blocks manager 40
Book Module functions
theme_book_admin_table 88
theme_book_export_html 88
theme_book_navigation 88

C

Color Module functions
theme_color_scheme_form 88

Comment Module functions
theme_comment 89
theme_comment_admin_overview 89
theme_comment_block 89
theme_comment_controls 89
theme_comment_flat_collapsed 89
theme_comment_flat_expanded 89
theme_comment_folded 89
theme_comment_post_forbidden 89
theme_comment_post_preview 89
theme_comment_thread_collapsed 89
theme_comment_thread_expanded 89
theme_comment_view 89
theme_comment_wrapper 89
common form issues, Drupal
data labels, form_alter() used 214
data labels, function overriding 215
data labels, modifying 214
data labels, new template creating 215
data labels, node adding 215, 216
images, using for buttons 217, 218
styling of form, form_alter() used 217
styling of form, function overriding 217
styling of form, modifying 216
styling of form, new template creating 217
CSS adapting, Tao theme
colors, setting 137, 138
comments, formatting 143
font styles, setting 137, 138
footer, formatting 141
form, formatting 143
horizontal menu, formatting 142
menus, formatting 141
new regions, formatiing 136
output, formatting 143

page dimensions, setting 136
search box, formatting 142
sidebars, formatting 141
vertical menu, formatting 142

D

default forms, Drupal
default contact forms 223
Poll module forms 228
Poll module forms, Poll Block Form 229
Poll module forms, Poll Page Form 229
search form, Advanced Search Form 227
search form, Block Search Form 226
search form, Page Search Form 226
search form, search results page 228
search form, Theme Search Form 225
search form, versions 224
search forms 224
user forms 219
user forms, Edit User Info Form 222
user forms, Login Block Form 219
user forms, Login Forms 219
user forms, Login Page Form 220
user forms, Request Password Form 221
user forms, User Registration Form 220
Dreamweaver 120
Drupal
additional theme, finding 25
additional theme, installing 28
common form issues 214
CSS overrides, working 103, 104
default CSS, overriding 101, 102
default form 218
form functions 203
form functions, Login Form 204, 205
form functions, modifying 206
form functions, override creating 204
form functions, overriding 206
forms, working 203
intercepts 16, 101
overrides 16, 101
overriding functions 105
template files, intercepting 116, 117
themeable functions, identifying 86
Drupal distro
about 17

concepts 17, 20
themes 17, 20
Drupal Module functions
theme_client_list 90
Drupal style sheets
about 83
admin.css 84
admin.css, selectors 231
aggregator.css 84
aggregator.css, selectors 232
block.css 84
block.css, selectors 232
book.css 84
book.css, selectors 232
color.css 84
color.css, selectors 233
comment.css 84
comment.css, selectors 233
default.css 85
default.css, selectors 233
farbtastic.css 85
farbtastic.css, selectors 234
forum.css 85
forum.css, selectors 234
held.css 85
held.css, selectors 234
locale.css 85
locale.css, selectors 235
maintenance.css 85
maintenance.css, selectors 235
node.css 85
node.css, selectors 235
poll.css 85
poll.css, selectors 236
search.css 85
search.css, selectors 236
selectors 231
style.css 86
system.css 86
system.css, selectors 237
tracker.css 86
tracker.css, selectors 238
user.css 86
user.css, selectors 238
watchdog.css 86
watchdog.css, selectors 238

Drupal theme
about 5, 6
blocks 9, 10
building 149, 151
files 21, 22
flexibility 7, 8
key concepts 12
modules 14
page, displaying 10-12
PHPTemplate theme, files 22, 23
pure PHP theme, files 23, 24
range 7, 8
regions 9, 10
significance 12
uninstalling 60
dynamic theming, PHPTemplate theme
about 185
CSS styling, creating 191
different template, using for group of
    pages 188
dynamic selectors, using for nodes 192
elements, associating with front page 189
multiple templates, using 186
page elements 189
section template, multiple templates
    using 186
selector, changing 192
separate admin theme, multiple templates
    using 186
specific template, assigning to a specific
    page 188
specific template, designating to a specific
    user 189
styling blocks 190, 191
styling modules 190, 191
styling nodes 191
unique homepage template, creating 188

E

existing theme, modifying
about 119
modifications, planning 120, 121
theme, cloning 122, 123
workspace, setting up 119, 120

F

Filter Module functions
theme_filter_admin_order 90
theme_filter_admin_overview 90
theme_filter_tips 90
theme_filter_tips_more_info 90
Form functions
theme_button 90
theme_checkbox 90
theme_checkboxes 90
theme_date 91
theme_fieldset 91
theme_file 91
theme_form 91
theme_form_element 91
theme_hidden 91
theme_item 91
theme_markup 91
theme_password 91
theme_password-confirm 91
theme_radio 91
theme_radios 91
theme_select 92
theme_textarea 91
theme_textfield 92
theme_token 92
form functions, Drupal
block templates 212
custom templates, creating 211
form_alter(), using 207-209
HTML, adding via function attributes 207
overriding, from template.php 209, 210
page templates 211
templates for form output 213
Forum functions
theme_forum_display 92
theme_forum_icon 92
theme_forum_list 92
theme_forum_topic_list 92
theme_forum_topic_navigation 92
functional elements, PHPTemplate theme
breadcrumb trail, main content area 162
content Region, main content area 164
feed icons, footer 164

footer 164
footer Region, footer 165
header region, header wrapper 161
header wrapper 159
help, main content area 163
logo, header wrapper 159
main content area, main wrapper 162
main wrapper 162
messages, main content area 163
primary links, inserting 161
secondary links, inserting 159
sidebar left, main wrapper 162
sidebar right, main wrapper 164
site mission, header wrapper 161
site name, header wrapper 160
site slogan, header wrapper 160
tabs, main content area 163
template closing tag, inserting 165
theme search box, header wrapper 160
title, main content area 163

K

key concepts, Drupal theme
  blocks, building with 14, 16
  intercept 16
  multiple themes 13
  override 16

L

Locale functions
  theme_locale_admin_manage_screen 92

M

Menu functions
  theme_menu_item 93
  theme_menu_item_link 93
  theme_menu_links 93
  theme_menu_local_task 93
  theme_menu_tree 93
module manager 38
modules
  managing 38

N

Node Module functions
  theme_node_admin_nodes 93
  theme_node_filter_form 93
  theme_node_filters 93
  theme_node_form 93
  theme_node_list 93
  theme_node_log_message 94
  theme_node_preview 94
  theme_node_search_admin 94

O

overrides, Drupal
  approaches 111
  Garland theme, PHPTemplate files
      intercepting 109
  Garland theme, themeable functions 110
  Garland theme, working 108
overriding fuctions, Drupal
  overrides, approaches 111
  overrides, naming 107
  overrides, placing 106

P

page.tpl.php file, PHPTemplate theme
  <body> tag, inserting 157
  <head> tag, inserting 156
  DocType, inserting 156
  functional elements, placing 158
  layout 158
  raw page.tpl.php file 165-168
Pagination functions
  theme_pager 94
  theme_pager_last 94
  theme_pager_link 94
  theme_pager_list 94
  theme_pager_next 94
  theme_pager_previous 94
PHP
  adding, to blocks 45
PHPTemplate
  about 61
  contrasting examples 77

Gagarin, PHPTemplate theme 78
Garland, PHPTemplate theme 78
key files 65
PHPTemplate file 71
PHPTemplate file, example 71-76
theme engine files 66
working 62-65
PHPTemplate theme
about 22
building 152
extending 179
functional elements, placing 158
new theme 178
page.tpl.php file, building 153, 155
style.css file 169
PHPTemplate theme, extending
additional variables 185
dynamic theming 185
template variables, working with 179
variables, intercepting 184
variables, overidding 184
variables in block.tpl.php 179, 180
variables in box.tpl.php 180
variables in comment.tpl.php 181
variables in node.tpl.php 181
variables in page.tpl.php 182
Poll Module functions
theme_poll_bar 95
theme_poll_results 95
theme_poll_view_voting 95
Profile Module functions
theme_profile_block 95
theme_profile_listing 95
pure PHP theme
building 193
pure PHP theme, building
document header 196
features, favIcon 196
features, implementing 196
features, logo 197
features, site name 197
features, site slogan 197
footer 200
HTML headers 196
main content area 199
main content area, breadcrumb trail 199
main content area, content Region 200

main content area, help 199
main content area, messages 200
main content area, tabs 199
main content area, title 199
overriding functions 201
primary links 198
secondary links 198
sidebar left 198
sidebar right 199
sidebars 198
theme.engine, elements 194
theme_features(), features 195
theme_features(), theme.engine functions 194
theme_regions(), theme.engine functions 194, 195
theme course 200

S

Search Module functions
theme_search_block_form 95
theme_search_item 95
theme_search_page 95
theme_search_theme_form 95
System Module functions
theme_admin_block 96
theme_admin_block_content 96
theme_admin_page 96
theme_system_admin_by_module 96
theme_system_modules 96
theme_system_modules_uninstall 96
theme_system_theme_select_form 96
theme_system_themes 96

T

Tao theme
about 123
configuring 127
CSS 123
CSS adapting 135
themeable functions 126
themeable functions, adapting 144
Tao theme, configuring
blocks, assigning to regions 134
blocks, configuring 133
blocks, enabling 133

changes, saving 129
dummy content, creating 129
global configuration settings 128
menus, setting up 129, 130
modules, enabling 128
new regions, adding 131, 132
theme configuration settings 128
user access setting 129
Taxonomy Module functions
theme_taxonomy_term_select 96
templating engine 6
theme, configuring
about 32, 47, 48
access levels, setting 54
blocks, managing 53
block visibility, setting 56-59
color picker, theme-specific configuration
    options 34
color scheme, setting 48
custom block, creating 55
display settings, changing 49
enable/disable page elements,
    theme-specific configuration
    options 35
favicon settings, theme-specific
    configuration options 36
global configuration 50
global configuration settings 37, 38
logo, uploading 50
logo settings, theme-specific configuration
    options 36
modules, enabling 52
theme-specific configuration options 33
themeable functions
Aggregator Module functions 87
Block Module functions 88
Book Module functions 88
Color Module functions 88
Comment Module functions 88
Drupal Module functions 90
Filter Module functions 90
Form functions 90
Forum Module functions 92
identifying 86
Locale functions 92
Menu functions 93
Node Module functions 93

Pagination functions 94
Poll Module functions 94
Profile Module functions 95
Search Module functions 95
System Module functions 96
Taxonomy Module functions 96
Theme Module functions 97
Upload Module functions 99
User Module functions 99
Watchdog Module functions 100
themeable functions, Tao theme
template.php, modifying 144
template file, creating 145, 146
theme engine files, PHPTemplate
block.tpl.php 66
box.tpl.php 67
comment.tpl.php 67
default.tpl.php 67
node.tpl.php 68
theme engines
alternative theme engines 80
installing 82
PHPTAL 80
PHPTemplate 61
PHP XTemplate 81
Smarty 81
Theme functions
theme_block 97
theme_blocks 97
theme_box 97
theme_breadcrumb 97
theme_closure 97
theme_feed_icon 97
theme_get_setting 97
theme_help 97
theme_image 97
theme_install_page 97
theme_item_list 97
theme_links 97
theme_maintenance_page 98
theme_mark 98
theme_more_help_link 98
theme_node 98
theme_page 98
theme_placeholder 98
theme_process_bar 98
theme_status_messages 98

theme_submenu 98
theme_table 98
theme_table_select_header_cell 98
theme_tablesort_indicator 98
theme_username 98
theme_xml_icon 98

U

Upload Module functions
theme_upload_attachments 99
theme_upload_form_current 99
theme_upload_form_new 99
User Module functions
theme_user_admin_account 99
theme_user_admin_new_role 99
theme_user_admin_perm 99
theme_user_filter_form 99
theme_user_filters 99

theme_user_list 99
theme_user_picture 99
theme_user_profile 99

W

Watchdog Module functions
theme_watchdog_form_overview 100

Z

Zen theme
about 120, 123
changes, implementing 121
cloning 122
CSS 123
CSS files 124
themeable functions 126
turning into Tao theme 127

Thank you for buying
Drupal 5 Themes

Packt Open Source Project Royalties

When we sell a book written on an Open Source project, we pay a royalty directly to that project. Therefore by purchasing Drupal 5 Themes, Packt will have given some of the money received to the Drupal Project.

In the long term, we see ourselves and you—customers and readers of our books—as part of the Open Source ecosystem, providing sustainable revenue for the projects we publish on. Our aim at Packt is to establish publishing royalties as an essential part of the service and support a business model that sustains Open Source.

If you're working with an Open Source project that you would like us to publish on, and subsequently pay royalties to, please get in touch with us.

Writing for Packt

We welcome all inquiries from people who are interested in authoring. Book proposals should be sent to authors@packtpub.com. If your book idea is still at an early stage and you would like to discuss it first before writing a formal book proposal, contact us; one of our commissioning editors will get in touch with you.

We're not just looking for published authors; if you have strong technical skills but no writing experience, our experienced editors can help you develop a writing career, or simply get some additional reward for your expertise.

About Packt Publishing

Packt, pronounced 'packed', published its first book "Mastering phpMyAdmin for Effective MySQL Management" in April 2004 and subsequently continued to specialize in publishing highly focused books on specific technologies and solutions.

Our books and publications share the experiences of your fellow IT professionals in adapting and customizing today's systems, applications, and frameworks. Our solution-based books give you the knowledge and power to customize the software and technologies you're using to get the job done. Packt books are more specific and less general than the IT books you have seen in the past. Our unique business model allows us to bring you more focused information, giving you more of what you need to know, and less of what you don't.

Packt is a modern, yet unique publishing company, which focuses on producing quality, cutting-edge books for communities of developers, administrators, and newbies alike. For more information, please visit our website: www.PacktPub.com.

Printed in the United States
106056LV00004B/131-134/A

9 781847 191823